THE TOTAL NOBODY
Who
Ran
FOR OFFICE
and
Lost
(ish)

SILKY

JOSHI MALIK

TRUE STORIES FROM MY FAILED BID FOR US CONGRESS

I have tried to recreate events, locales, and conversations from my memories of them. In some instances, I have changed the names of individuals and places in order to maintain their anonymity, and I may have changed some identifying characteristics and details such as physical properties, occupations, and places of residence.

Paperback: 978-1-7355693-0-7
Ebook: 978-1-7355693-1-4

Library of Congress Number: 2020917055
First paperback edition October 2020

Edited by Daniel J. Cohen and Alexander Oriani
Cover art by David Drummond
Interior Layout by Julie Karen Hodgins
Author photograph by Abigail Quan
All other photographs courtesy of Silky Joshi Malik

Printed by IngramSpark in the U.S.A.

Terrier Publishing House
Houston, TX 77098
TerrierPublishingHouse.com

SilkyJMalik.com

To Imran, for always being my biggest fan
and my loudest cheerleader, especially when
I do crazy shit like run for Congress

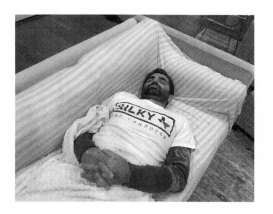

CONTENTS

FOREWORD

"…The lesson for aspiring elected officials is simple. Even successful politicians sometimes lose elections.

The editorial board has spent the past few months interviewing scores of candidates who took the initiative to run for public office. Even if they had no hope of winning, even if their qualifications have been questionable, their commitment has been inspiring…

We met some mighty impressive citizens who put their reputations on the line and their names on the ballot but ended up losing their primaries. Indeed, many of them faced such stiff competition they didn't even win our endorsement. But some of them have been so compelling we want to encourage them to stay in politics. They deserve a second mention, because we hope we see their names on the ballot again in the future …

Silky Malik walks and talks like the future of the Democratic Party in Houston. She's a Montrose resident with an MBA from Texas A&M who ran in the primary for the congressional seat now occupied by Ted Poe. She's lively and smart and she speaks with uncommon passion, particularly when she explains why millennial voters are looking for honest and authentic candidates who won't sell them out to special interests. 'I think we can have leaders who inspire people the way FDR inspired me,' she told us.

Silky Malik, please run again."

—The Houston Chronicle
March 8, 2018

KEEPING
IT *Real*

I t took me nearly three months of writing this book before I could begin writing it honestly. I'm not sure why that is, at least not totally. Reading through the first iteration of my chapters left me thoroughly uninterested in what I was reading. Everything on those pages was sterile and Pollyanna-ish; for some reason, I had been self-censoring my stories and accounts, perhaps in the hopes of writing a "serious, grown-up" book. Being contrived and worried about what others might think of me was an unexpected feeling, mainly because for most of my life, and much to the chagrin of my very Indian and Pakistani immigrant family, I have always been an open book, and a far too open one at that. Probably because I don't like keeping secrets. Secrets feel like lies.

I'm like a five-year-old that wants you to know everything about her even if you don't care or didn't ask. So long as a question isn't sexist, shitty, or inappropriate, I can be counted on to answer it honestly. I remember being a kid, answering the phone to "Hello Silky. Is your mom there?" while my mom gave me the classic 'I'm not here' gesture, and me, eight years old and WEAK, buckling under the pressure of having to lie to someone, sheepishly replying "Yes, auntie. Here she is", and just handing the phone over to my mom while avoiding eye contact like the coward I was.

Being candid and honest is easy and natural for me, but writing a book has been less so. Though I spent my youth and adolescence journaling and writing very bad, very angsty poetry, setting out to "write a book" has, at times, been arduous and emotionally taxing. I'm not entirely sure why that is. I think part of it is that I've totally gotten into my own head about all of this. This book *that no one is forcing me to write*—a project that was *supposed t*o be fun and *maybe* helpful to people someday down the road—has instead been hard and super not fun. On my first attempt at writing this book of essays, I was painstakingly hesitant and cautious with my words—with the truth—when that's not who I've ever been in real life. After hearing my editors politely imply that my stories might be less boring if I were less filtered, I realized I needed to just feel my feelings. The irony of being told by anyone to be *less* filtered is not lost on me, considering that until I was about thirty years old I had two settings: silent or shameless. The shameless setting got me into trouble on a weekly basis.

For a long while, possibly most of my adulthood, I've carried with me this internalized feeling of being a disappointment. I was *supposed* to become a doctor or engineer or something equally stable, responsible, and respectable. I had *potential*, but instead, I chose to study liberal arts in college like some damn HIPPIE, and now, I wanted to become a public servant. What kind of Indian girl runs for office! It's bad enough I didn't become some high-rolling, money-making professional. Was I also going to possibly embarrass myself *and* my family by being completely transparent about myself and my beliefs, publicly showing both in an unflattering light? Did my parents immigrate to America forty years ago only to have their good name besmirched, and their dirty laundry aired?

With all this "don't air your dirty laundry" making itself at home in the back of my mind, when I began writing about my experience running for office, I unknowingly convinced myself to write about the stuff that makes me look good. I would portray myself as extra witty and urbane. My readers would aspire to be just like me: a woman of the world, dignified and poised, the walking embodiment of grace under fire. Instead of Whataburger and Diet Coke, I'd recount how I had charmed the who's who of Houston, champagne flute in one hand, and cigarette, placed in its long, skinny, silver holder, in the other. I've never seen a cigarette holder in real life, and actually, I don't even smoke, but you get the idea: me, cool, somehow inhaling smoke without coughing up a lung, and effortlessly chic.

The funny thing is I know it's the raw and unflattering stuff that actually makes someone look good and makes their experiences worth reading. No one wants to read about the perfect person who has their life entirely together and never misses a beat, all the while maintaining a successful career, family, social life, a trim waistline, and a healthy diet. We want to know about the rookie congressional candidate eating cold Taco Bell burritos because she's too exhausted to care and hates her life. That's the charming and relatable stuff folks want to read, right?

Emotional baggage aside, I recognize that I am worried about looking stupid to the political community I've spent nearly three years trying to break into and earn the respect of. As an emotionally well-adjusted person would say, let's unpack this.

Before running for Congress, I was a total political nobody. A mysterious ingénue, I ran because I wanted to change the world and shake things up. What did I have to lose?

I didn't know the who's who of Houston's political and donor class. I didn't know the activists or groups around Houston (and Texas). I had no one to impress except for the voters. And that felt like a task I could handle.

It didn't take me long to realize I had no idea what the hell I was doing. I remember walking into big rooms filled with fancy, important people, most of whom knew each other, and feeling so painfully, obviously, out of place—a total interloper. Like some tacky-ass mofo in a Banana Republic Outlet blazer who was crashing the event and sticking out like a sore thumb.

After I ran and lost, something unexpected happened. The morning after losing my primary election, the Houston Chronicle gave me an incredibly kind shout-out. Out of the nearly 300 Democratic primary candidates running in Harris County, the third-largest county in the US, only eight of us were asked, in print, to "please, run again."

I was fully expecting to feel like a total loser after the election. Coming in third felt shitty. Being unable to fundraise enough to get into a runoff felt shitty. I assumed everyone would think I was a joke because I lost. Running myself ragged on the campaign trail, I didn't have time to stop and think of all the great things we were doing. But when that op-ed came out, I felt pride in what my team and I had accomplished. There, in black and white, in one of the largest newspapers in Texas, I was told I was awesome and was asked to run again.

★

I've always been an edgy non-conformist who refuses to even *want* to be part of any cool clubs (can I blame this on being an Aries?). I literally didn't see the original Jurassic Park until, like, 2016, because despite being *obsessed* with dinosaurs as a kid, when the movie came out, everyone was *so* into it and, to be honest, just kinda weird about forcefully telling others nonstop, "You just HAVE to go see it!" that my gut reaction was, "Ew. Why would I go see it just because everyone else is going to see it?" I missed out on an epic movie that I wanted to see just because of my irrational desire to be nOn-CoNfOrMiSt!

When I decided to run for office, I was constantly aware of my outsider status. Even though the politics of 2016 meant that all bets were off and literally ANYONE could become a politician now, there was still some awkwardness to be felt by those of us stepping into the arena for the first time in our lives. But in 2018 things changed again in our country's politics. Outsiders won the day and helped us take back the House. AOC and The Squad proved that people over politics was the name of the game; being a nobody running for office, hoping to make a difference because you're tired of the bullshit wasn't edgy and different. It was cool and patriotic.

I wasn't part of the wave of progressive Democratic women and people of color (POC) elected to the House of Representatives in 2018, but I did get to be part of the fabric of history in my home state by being the first Indian woman to run for Congress in Texas. And after the Chronicle's post-election pep talk, it felt like I was no longer an outsider, but the face of what governance in Texas and the US should and would look like someday.

A lot of us nobodies accidentally created our own cool kids political club. And now that I was kinda in it, I sure as hell wasn't gonna get myself kicked out!

Y'all, being liked is a hell of a drug.

Interestingly enough, the flipside of feeling like a joke or a loser isn't as great as I thought it would be. When you're an outsider who's crashing the party, the expectations are kinda low. Please don't eat all the shrimp. Please don't break and/or steal anything. And ... that's pretty much it. Apparently, though, when you realize people have some respect for your moxie and pluck, and that they think you might be *going places*, a new feeling takes over:

Fear.

Fear that you might prove everyone wrong. Fear that you'll become a disappointment who lets people down. Fear that *actually* you're not cool at all, and that *actually* all your moxie, pluck, and gumption was just you winging it, and that, yeah, maybe you're not *actually* going places.

But, I'm also afraid of mucking it up for everyone else.

It's easy for women and minorities to be written off and dismissed if they aren't good or perfect enough. How unfiltered am I allowed to be before I make us all look stupid? If my book is too honest and all you see is me—a regular woman who ran for office solely because she felt it was the moral thing to do; who was unpolished, relatively unprepared, and unfunded; who was mostly winging it and relying on her instincts and lost her race—would it help or hurt the cause? Would I get kicked out of the club? Would it make other newcomers trying to break into politics look stupid? Would keeping it 100 and putting myself out there make me look like a joke?

Nah. Fuck that.

What's the point of trying to change the world if we can't keep it real?

At the risk of getting a stern talking to from my very Indian mom for "airing my dirty laundry," and possibly being disowned for three weeks, I'd say keeping it 100 with y'all is worth it, so that's what I'm gonna do.

Sorry in advance for cursing too much, Mom. <3

LEE

I ran for Congress because I lost a bar bet. Well, not exactly, but that's how my friend and campaign policy adviser, Lee, likes to tell the story. Writing an entire chapter on Lee will only make him more insufferable than he already is. But for better or worse, Lee is not only one of the smartest people I've ever met, he's now one of my best friends and is also an integral part of this story. And the way he tells it, I ran for Congress because I lost a bar bet to him.

There's a popular statistic that states that, on average, it takes asking a woman to run for office at least seven times before she considers doing it. I, however, immediately *told* seven people I would run for office the second I decided to run.

I can even remember the very first time I mentioned wanting to run for office to someone other than my husband. It was 2015, and I'd just moved back to Houston after three years of living in Southeast Asia. While waiting for final approval to become a substitute teacher with the Houston Independent School District, I started a retail job at the Loft store near my house so that I could take advantage of their sweet, sweet fifty percent off employee discount. Demarcus, the store manager, and I were organizing the sale section at the back of the store, hanging clothes up by color in anticipation of a big "sale is on sale" weekend coming up. We were consumed with horror at the ongoing news coverage of the presidential race. Though it feels like 500 years ago, the news cycle was pretty batshit crazy by 2015 standards, and none of us had ever seen anything like it.

Flailing last season's blouses around in anger, I proclaimed to Demarcus that I was tired of all these rich, old, white guys being in charge of everything and vowed, "I'm totally going to run for office someday!"

We'd only known each other for a couple of months, but he gave me a high five and the biggest, best, most encouraging "Hell yeah. That's my girl!" a person could want. His enthusiasm made me feel less sheepish about wanting to pursue something so ... different than who I thought I was. For the rest of my time at Loft, Demarcus proudly bragged to everyone about how I was planning to run for office someday. He was my hype man, and to this day, I am grateful for his knee-jerk show of faith and support. So for the next two years, I did what I could to learn about politics, all while continuing to casually tell folks I was going to run for office "someday."

Dipping my toe into local politics in early 2016, I applied to an open board position with the City of Sugar Land to be on the Land Use Advisory Committee. A month later, they sent me an email saying that I had been accepted! Showing up to meetings every month to discuss the future of the city and talking about how to improve things was a really cool feeling. I felt like the poster child for how to be a good citizen.

I then began attending various neighborhood-type meetings around town. If a group of involved suburban locals and concerned citizens were meeting up to talk about fining people for having dead grass in their front yard or whether or not the fences were high enough, I tried to make sure I was there. Whenever I met someone who seemed political-y, I'd ask them for advice about which other civic or political groups I could join. Before exiting any conversation, I would casually throw in an awkward "Um hey! How does a person run for office?"

I phone banked and canvassed (or "block walked," as we say in Texas) for candidates in adjacent counties, and went to meetings in the houses and apartments of strangers hoping to make a friend or two that could teach me about politics. One day, I showed up to a Young Dems club meeting held at Rice University, completely unaware it was meant for Rice students only. Shortly after realizing it was a *student* club and that I was about fifteen years older than everyone in attendance, I pretended to take an important call out in the hallway and left. I'm still bitter over the ten dollars I paid for visitor parking.

Even here in MAGA-cap-red Texas, the 2016 election had us all shook.[1] After Trump and his fascist cronies took the White House, candidate trainings began to pop up all over the state. Tired of asking Google and strangers around Houston how exactly to go about running for office, I jumped at the opportunity to take a one-day Annie's List training on a Saturday in January 2017.

The random girl I plopped next to was so incredibly bubbly and kind. A recent college graduate, she was full of the perfect amount of youthful, unbridled enthusiasm and hope. To be honest, even though it had only been two months since the

---

1   Hey young readers, this book is hip! Tell your friends!

November 2016 election, the entire union hall of about sixty women was bristling with excitement and positivity. Our country was now being run by a psychopath, and we weren't going to sit around while the world went to shit. We were there to learn how to #resist, and it was an awesome day.

When Sara, the girl next to me, asked which office I was planning on running for, without hesitation (or much thought) I said, "Oh, U.S. Senator. But, like, when I'm forty or something."

To her credit, she tried very hard to hide the surprise and doubt from her face, and I *almost* couldn't tell she thought I was insane, naive, or both. Nevertheless, Sara remarked that while she thought U.S. Senator was an awesome aspiration, she didn't see a woman, especially a Democratic woman of color, winning in Texas for at least another twenty years, and that I'd "probably have better luck if [I] moved to a bluer state." She wasn't being shitty, just pragmatic. I knew she was right. Flipping a U.S. Senate seat in Texas would be difficult, and considering I was a know-nothing nobody,[2] I probably needed to set my sights a little bit lower. So I decided to start small; I'd run for Congress instead.

That day-long Annie's List training was just the beginning, and not long after, I applied for a summer fellowship with Battleground Texas. This group of twenty people, many of whom had incredibly impressive bios and resumes, was my real introduction to politics. My weekend crash course in politics

---

2 Being a know-nothing nobody is very advantageous in that you don't know enough to be scared to reach for something too big or impracticable.

with BGTX helped me solidify, internally, that I was going to definitely run for office someday.

One of the more memorable exercises from that weekend was breaking off into groups and running a mock campaign that we had to build and run from scratch. Each group member took on a role: campaign manager, field director, communications director, and candidate. Impulsively, I volunteered to be the candidate, and we set to work on our campaign. I began writing a stump speech and asked my team their thoughts on what our slogan should be. I decided it would be a great idea if our campaign reclaimed American patriotism, something along the lines of *Vote Silky for America, Vote Democrat for the American Dream*. Kinda cheesy, I know, but why should Republicans have the market cornered on Life, Liberty, and the American Dream?

After two hours of working on my pitch, I walked up to the front of the room, confident and poised. I knew I had this. I started to deliver my stump speech. Rather, I attempted to deliver my stump speech only to realize, midway through my first sentence, that I couldn't hear what the hell I was even saying because all I *could* hear was an ocean's worth of blood rushing through my ears.

I'd spent years doing debate, working as a teacher, presenting research studies, and conducting health education with patients. I loved talking to people! I was also really good at it. This would be my moment of self-affirmation, proof I was *destined* for public office. An Indian, female Barack Obama, full of swagger, effortlessly wooing my audience with visions of a brighter tomorrow while my words filled them with hope and purpose.

However, in my brain, *giving a campaign speech* is filed right alongside *how to outrun a bear*. I'd completely forgotten about my stage fright right up until the moment I was in front of a group of practical strangers, cosplaying an inspiring candidate for office, and failing to do so in spectacular fashion. Just peachy. Blathering on for my allotted five minutes, my voice unsteady and deaf to the words coming out of my mouth, and going completely off-script, I said nothing remarkable or important. Our group did not win the campaign competition that weekend. Shocking, I know.

Considering I ended up doing another two candidate trainings that year, clearly I was undeterred. Or a glutton for punishment. Same, same.

In Spring of 2017, a few months before meeting Lee, I had been going around town casually mentioning to people (none of whom asked) that I was thinking of running in the Democratic primary against Congressman Ted Poe. At the time, I wasn't really involved with the local party and was still getting to know the ins and outs of Houston's political scene. I was a member of several now-defunct groups trying to organize and #resist the new president. I certainly wasn't announcing my intention to run in 2020 to any politicos or folks "in the know." Nope. I was telling only my friends and family (and a stranger I was seated next to at an Annie's List luncheon). Everyone I told was politely supportive; it was kind of like telling your grandparents about how awesome you are at *Pokemon Go* and being given unconditional love and support despite them having no idea wtf you're talking about.

At the time, the women's political activism group that I was part of had decided to host an event at Axelrad, a really cool bar known for hosting Houston's liberals: completely outdoors (a nightmare in the summer for prissy folks like me), gravel everywhere (don't wear sandals), a standing-room-only pizza place with the best pizza in Houston (off to the side, but not part of Axelrad), adorable dogs in bandanas (with their Instafamous-looking owners), and beer (from several of our local breweries). Definitely a hipster's paradise, and I say that with affection because I like to talk up Houston's hipster scene lest my readers falsely believe Austin is the only liberal city in Texas!

Our little political group decided to help get out the vote for a progressive woman running for the school board in what was quickly becoming a hotly contested race. We invited Elizabeth—first time political candidate, a true progressive, and a young woman of color—to come meet potential voters and give her spiel. Members of our club then drove voters to the polls.

It was Halloween, and the bar was hosting a doggie costume contest as well. Because Houstonians spend all year longing for the crispness of fall, nearly every person there was wearing boots, a puffer jacket, and/or a flannel shirt even though it was, like, sixty-seven degrees that day. The bar was packed, and we were ready to drive some souls to the polls!

Only four or five women from our group were able to make it out, and we set up shop on a picnic table near the front entrance so that patrons could easily see the candidate's signage as soon as they walked in. We were hoping to foster a sense of community with this event and make voting with like-minded progressives feel like a fun, hip thing to do on a beautiful afternoon. You know, building community and promoting civic engagement like the trailblazing suffragettes before us! #BeInspired #BeTheChange

Instead, what we got was disappointed dog owners coming over to us to register their pets dressed as Snow White, Yoda, and the Pope for the costume contest. When Lee walked up to our table with his dog Kiwi, a beautiful brown and white Australian Shepherd with adorable floppy ears, I immediately assumed he was participating in the costume contest and directed him to the registration table. Half laughing at me with confusion on his face, he gave me a very polite side-eye and instead went over to greet his friend and the president of our org, Eryn.

I spent a few minutes talking to Elizabeth about her time on the trail. She was a high school teacher fed up with how the kids in her school and the district were being underserved. Despite being a total political noob and outsider with no estab-lishment support, she decided to step up. Elizabeth seemed like she was running on fumes, but she was clearly not going down without one hell of a fight. I found her run and our short conversation to be interesting and inspiring.

Something only a person with hearing loss might not know is that I am a really loud person, and I tend to gravitate toward other loud people, probably because it lets me feel like I'm soft-spoken and ladylike in comparison. Lee might be even louder than I am. He's also half a foot taller than me and has a pretty imposing presence. Because he was being super loud, I knew we'd get along swell, so I walked over to talk to him. Also, the woman he was talking to sort of looked like she could use some rescuing from the loud conversation he was having with her, seemingly against her will. Like the noble, heroic conversation buffer no one needed or asked for, I swooped in and jumped right into a conversation I wasn't asked to join. Clearly, I've still got that awkwardly clueless middle school swag, y'all!

Lee: So are all of you ladies here planning on running for office?

Me: No. Most of us aren't … I don't think. I am, though. In 2020. For Congress.

Lee: What district do you live in?

Me: Two. Ted Poe's district.

Lee: Ha! The one with all the dudes running and no women?

Me: Wait. I thought there was a woman in that race? Or someone was planning on jumping in?

Lee: Nope. That's CD7. CD2 is a total sausage fest. You should run! I'll even help you!

Me: Ha. Okay, dude. I'm actually running in 2020.

Lee: No, I'm serious. You should run now. If the 2018 blue wave hits like it's supposed to, a Dem could flip the seat.

Me, trying to politely back out of this conversation with this strange man aggressively trying to convince me to run for Congress: Um, yeah, I'll think about it!

Deranged Lee: Hey, let's exchange numbers and do lunch next week so you can't blow me off. I think you should run this cycle, and I bet when I show you the numbers it'll convince you.

Thankfully, his partner Margaret walked up to us just as I was about to start screaming "stranger danger!" Her slight frame and extremely calm energy and demeanor was a reassuring contrast to Lee's and eased my fears that he was a serial killer who crashes grassroots political events around the country in the hopes of securing a nonstop supply of naive, politically idealistic victims.

Less than three days later, over sandwiches and Linzer cookies at Paulie's, Lee convinced me to run for Congress, two years ahead of schedule.

I waited nearly five weeks after that lunch to see whether a woman would announce that she was running in the Democratic primary. I figured that, hey, if another woman runs, I'm totally off the hook, and I can just chill and bide my time for the next two years.

No such luck.

About six weeks after losing that bet to probable-serial-killer Lee, I formally announced my candidacy for the U.S. House of Representatives, Texas's Second Congressional District.

Typically, a campaign kickoff party is held at a restaurant or a venue somewhere in the district. An unspoken rule dictates that the establishment should be home-grown and local. No chain restaurants, please! I decided that the best place to have my kickoff would be at the Black Labrador Pub, a beloved local restaurant that had served the Montrose neighborhood, where I currently live, for more than thirty-three years. It was also where I had my twenty-fourth birthday party. Ten years later, I was back—this time in the jazz lounge upstairs, setting up for my congressional kickoff.

Dim, older, and larger than I remembered it being a decade prior, the room had a musty neighborhood charm, making it exactly what I wanted for such an important night. I have always been drawn to restaurants that are unassuming and don't feel a need to put on airs. Places that give off a Cheers vibe—anyone's welcome, and we'll all know your name by the time you leave. I like to think that's who I am as both a person and a candidate: unassuming and welcoming.[3]

Without a full campaign staff in place, it was all hands on deck, even though it was mostly just my friends and family. The Silky Squad got to the Black Lab a little over an hour early to set up. Chelsea, in charge of communications and PR, volunteered to help collect donations; she assured me that no one could turn down a *very* pregnant lady asking for money. She was right. Out of everyone who volunteered to collect donations, she ended up collecting the highest amount by the

---

3   But not necessarily musty and larger than one might recall, haha.

end of the night. Courtney, Lee, Imran, Brenda, my brother Shane, and my mom, were all tasked with one thing or the other. Courtney and Imran made sure to get all the tables set up and our sign-in station ready to go. That night, we debuted my brand new campaign t-shirts. Lemme tell you, seeing all these folks wearing a shirt with my name plastered across the front of it was truly surreal. Even today, whenever I see one of those shirts on someone, I still get the warm fuzzies.

After the cake was delivered, looking fly as hell emblazoned with my campaign logo, I suddenly became very aware of the possibility that I'd be giving my speech to an empty room. I turned to Imran.

"What if nobody shows up?"

He told me obviously that wasn't going to happen and not to worry. Filled with complete certainty that my party would be a bust, I was perspiring so profusely in my new red dress that were it not for my Spanx coming in clutch, my sweaty secret would have been quickly betrayed.

A month prior, at a candidate training in D.C., my long-lost stage fright had decided to reappear. After royally bombing my practice stump speech at that training, I realized memorizing speeches wasn't going to help me when I was so nervous that I felt like throwing up. The only way I could even begin to stand in front of a group of people and not immediately forget my entire speech was to speak with such brutal honesty about my lived experiences that there'd be practically no speech to memorize. I just needed to keep it real, yo.

I talked about growing up poor as the daughter of immigrants, with a dad who had his own business (and a drinking problem). Because his business wasn't profitable, times were often really lean for us. The few years before and after his death when I was twenty-one only stretched us more, taking me from one to two part-time jobs, and forcing my mom to work nearly seven days a week, taking every bit of overtime she could get.

Despite all of this, the American Dream wasn't necessarily out of our reach.

My brother and I were free lunch kids until we graduated high school. We were also Texas CHIP recipients, which meant our household income qualified us for government-subsidized healthcare/insurance well into college.

Later, I would qualify for enough need-based education scholarships, grants, and loans that I would be able to make it through state college.

Like so many Americans, I got where I was because my country didn't give up on me just because I was born in the wrong tax bracket or zip code. I was lucky enough to grow up in an America that saw value in all of its citizens and had programs in place to give each of us a fighting chance at our own American Dream.

A woman like me had no business running to be their next congresswoman, and history had shown us as much.

Nevertheless, there I was, doing the unlikely by virtue of what this country afforded me—my own shot at an American Dream of my choosing. And at that moment in history, I was doing my patriotic duty by standing up against the Trump administration, heeding a moral calling to do what was right, even if it was a little scary. This was my American Dream, and I was going after it no matter what.

Walking from one side of the room to the other, my throat fluttering, I held the audience's gaze and tried not to trip over my words.

Somehow, I didn't trip—metaphorically or literally.

Instead, I knocked it out of the freaking park. People applauded and then donated! Standing at the front of this room full of maybe sixty people, half of whom I didn't even know, I talked without pretense. For that six minutes, I was the person I had always wanted to see running for office: someone clearly full of flaws and lacking polish, but speaking with candor and heart about what life is like for lots of Americans. With my candidacy, I aimed to show the stark contrast between myself and the typical congressional hopeful. No Ivy League degrees, trust funds, or congressional internships here. Just a lotta bootstrapping, pluck, and enough headstrong optimism to believe, and show, that anyone can run for office.

It was the first time I'd ever really been upfront about parts of my upbringing being so financially strained. I imagine that most people don't like talking about growing up poor, and I was no exception. But it's a big reason I am who I am today, so I refused to shy away from it. The crowd went wild for me: the young, honest, normie-turned-politician in the making.

They liked me. They *really* liked me!

My mom, however, standing off to the side, arms crossed, was fighting back tears. Tears of joy maybe? Probably not. She did not look as though she liked me very much. Although I gave the audience my most real and authentic self, what I did not do was give my mom and brother a heads up about how I'd essentially be airing our family's dirty laundry to a room full of strangers. They were blindsided and embarrassed by my speech, and I had zero clue. Selfishly, it never occurred to me that my path to politics, *my* life story, could have anything to do with them.

Though she stayed the whole night, my mom left my congressional campaign kickoff party with little more than a tepid goodbye.

My mom and I have a complicated relationship at times. She has always been and will always be my biggest cheerleader (right after my husband), and she basically thinks the sun shines out of my ass. She's a huge reason why I have such obnoxiously high self-esteem and unwavering self-worth; she loves me so much, and knowing how loved I am has been foundational to my growth as a person. We are total opposites, though, in nearly every way, with the difference being more akin to fire and oxygen than yin and yang, making for a decidedly interesting and spirited adolescence wherein I endlessly practiced my debate skills on her, the unwilling participant that she was.

We had so many broke years as a family, and honest to God, if it wasn't for her selfless dedication to us and my dad, I don't know how a roof would have remained over our heads. It's easy to forget or discount the work and sacrifice of our parents because sometimes we get too wrapped up in ourselves. But I know with certainty, were it not for my mom working nonstop, at all kinds of weird hours for over two decades, I would not be where I am today.

I didn't know she was mad at me until the next day when she wouldn't answer my calls, forcing me to call my brother to figure out what was going on. Turns out the only thing more disappointing to an Asian parent than their child not becoming a doctor or an engineer is their child talking to a bunch of strangers about how they grew up poor. I had embarrassed her and my late father by denigrating our family to a crowd of strangers *and* my in-laws.

For the next few weeks, I called my mom every day only to be met with the silent treatment. I get it. She was hurt by her very disappointing Indian daughter's speech to a room full of randos that gave the appearance my brother and I grew up unloved, impoverished, and neglected.

In the end, only after the fourth time I showed up to her house and stood outside both arms outstretched and waving around wildly, pleading with her to love me again (her love language is Bollywood levels of public adoration), did she finally stop ghosting me. I lured her out of her apartment with the promise of dosas and chai at her favorite Indian restaurant. Not until our second styrofoam cup of chai did she explain how my kickoff speech painted her and my father as total and utter failures.

While my mom being hurt or caught off guard by my speech was valid, I also felt hurt.

Sure, I completely own that I was thoughtless and hurt her feelings, but she totally abandoned me in a moment of great need. I was in the middle of my very first campaign, doing something so out of my wheelhouse and a little bit scary, that having to do it without my mom's support (or physical presence) felt incredibly shitty.

★

When the people you've known your whole life—people who you'd give a literal damn vital organ to if they needed it—disappear during your campaign, you can't help but feel stranded and alone. You may even question your entire relationship and whether y'all were ever really friends. But the simple truth is that lots of people aren't interested in or cut out for politics. The abandoners love you and are silently rooting for you every step of the way, but they may not understand that you *also* need their help in the way of grunt work or money. This doesn't mean they don't care about you. They just aren't really going to be able to show you they care in any tangible way that will help your campaign. So, yes, they're kinda useless for now, but it's only temporary, I promise.

It can be hard to go back to how your life or relationships were before you ran. I remember constantly being both disappointed and pleasantly surprised by the help, or lack thereof, from people on my campaign. Sometimes the people you think you'll be able to count on are nowhere to be found.

On the flip side, there are people who will show up when you need them most, to cheer you on, lift you up, and get you over the finish line. My younger brother Shane, for instance, entertained attendees at my kickoff with his fantastic up-close magic. I didn't even ask him to do that. He just stepped up and decided the best way he could support his sister in that moment was keeping folks entertained before my speech started. He warmed up the crowd for me, and I'll always be grateful to him for that.

When I first told my mom I was running for Congress, her immediate reaction was "Wow. I'm so proud of you. You would be a great president, you know. You should run for that, someday."

Thanks, Mom.

CAN YOU DIE FROM *Embarrassment?*

P art of what makes the whole process of running for office so taxing is the different ways political junkies measure just how good or viable of a candidate you are. If you're not careful, these unsolicited opinions start to feel like a measurement of how good or viable of a *person* you are.

For uninitiated readers, viability is to your political campaign what potatoes are to your meal: reliable enough to be part of the dish, but not so amazing you're winning any Michelin stars with it as your main ingredient. Viability is political speak for someone who is the perfect amount of milquetoast so as to neither scare nor excite the electorate. If your candidate is too exciting, they might inspire folks to believe in and demand **REAL** change, which could threaten the status quo and those who benefit from it. If your candidate is too boring, no one will show up to vote for them, and you'll ensure a Republican victory.

Ultimately, viability is thinktank bullshit designed to help mediocrity secure a place at the top and instill doubt in first-time candidates. You might be walking around thinking you're awesome, but then your polling or quarterly fundraising numbers come in and they suck, so you immediately start to wonder whether they suck because *you* suck. On the day of my first fundraiser, I was pretty certain I was the suckiest congressional candidate that ever ran for office. Not because I didn't raise any money that night, but because practically no one showed up.

I was mere hours away from walking into my very first bona fide fundraiser at one of the nicest tribrid art galleries/interior design showrooms/furniture stores in Houston, Native Citizen. To underscore just how fancy I felt deep in my soul, I'd gone out and bought a whole new outfit: chic, blue velvet trousers with a beautiful champagne-colored silk blouse. If I was gonna be raising money for my campaign, I had better damn well look like money while doing it!

My staff and I felt confident about the ins and outs of facilitating a fundraiser—confidence owed mostly to the fact that all of us were newcomers to politics, giving us the advantage of being both completely clueless and endlessly positive about everything. Don't get me wrong. There is something very endearing about a ragtag group of noobies and nobodies working together for a cause they believe in. However, showing up to a fundraiser with maybe eight people in attendance, six of whom you're related to, feels like a lot of things, and endearing isn't one of them.

One of the best parts of my unsuccessful fundraiser was that the owner of Native Citizen, the amazing Denny, donated a work of art by resident artist Edgar Medina for attendees to bid on. I first met Denny a couple of years prior when scouring the city for a perfect coffee table. I stumbled upon Native Citizen tucked away in the heart of Montrose. The facade is unassuming but chic, and once inside you know you're walking out with something special for your home. If there's a place for everything, and everything has its place, at Native Citizen, everything is exactly where it should be, even if it shouldn't go there at all. Flooded with ridiculous amounts of natural light, the space feels like the working lab of some sort of genius. Overcome with this fabulous notion that you're hunting for treasure, you'll know X marks the spot only when something beautiful both catches your eye and makes your heart flutter. The day I bought my coffee table, a two-hundred-pound faded-yellow bomb carrier with a large round glass top, I also spent a few hours learning everything I could about the life of the artistic genius who made it. Denny, a lawyer-turned-designer with a heart of gold, has a quiet, fiery rebelliousness and tries to make the world a little bit better wherever he can. He spends untold hours volunteering his studio and his time for myriad causes around Houston. He also does cool shit like dismantle World War II fighter jets and turn them into things like chandeliers and coffee tables.

The piece Denny donated to my fundraiser was an abstract painting, vibrant and bold with lots of oranges and pinks of all shades. Looking at it felt like that first step outside into the bright sun after sitting at your desk in a freezing office all day. Edgar was on hand to talk with guests about his painting, making the event feel that much more special. It's just too bad no one was in attendance to bid on the damn thing.

About forty-five minutes into the event, it became clear no one else I wasn't related to was going to show up. I considered faking some sort of very vague, very catastrophic emergency to get the hell out of there. Maybe some casual arson by lighting one of Denny's beautiful reclaimed tweed couches on fire. Do judges go easy on first-time casual arsonists? Ultimately,

I decided to stay. I wasn't in this race to be a quitter who runs at the first sign of failure!

Also, Imran made me stay. Through a big smile, he whispered that I was not allowed to ditch my own event, even if I was in fact literally dying from embarrassment. So I worked the room of seven people (or was it ten people? Actually it may have been four people ... plus my ghost, since I'd already died from embarrassment an hour earlier) and we all had a lively, polite conversation for almost two hours. I see my family once a week, so there wasn't much new stuff for us to talk about since I'd seen them only a few days prior.

Since that night, I've often been struck with flashes of leftover embarrassment, and for a long time, I couldn't quite pinpoint why. I would be washing the dishes and *BAM* near-full trays of cheese and meat floating mid-air across my eyes. Walking the dogs and *BAM* unopened bottles of Trader Joe's wine doing somersaults while mocking me amidst beautiful art and furniture. *BAM* The videographer I'd hired for the night inconspicuously working to get good footage, but there's only eight of us, so he leaves an hour and a half early because he didn't want to waste my money filming an empty room. *BAM* Kill me now, please.

My failed fundraiser still lingers at the back of my mind because, at the time, it felt like it confirmed my biggest fears about running for Congress. During one of my candidate trainings, I recall being told "A good candidate will always be able to raise money." I may have been a nobody who was completely winging it, but damn, I didn't want to also look like a total joke utterly out of her element. When no one showed up to my first fundraiser, I took it as proof that I wasn't a good candidate and that I was making a fool out of myself doing something I had no business doing.

Since the end of my 2018 March primary election, I have attended an astounding number of fundraisers. To my surprise, there was one event where maybe five percent of the invited guest list showed up despite the candidate being politically viable. Watching the candidate make painful small talk with the handful of people in attendance, I wondered if she was feeling the same way I felt at my own failed fundraiser: embarrassed, unpopular, foolish, and out of her depths.

It is my sincerest hope that all candidates and elected officials have events where no one shows up and they end up feeling super lame and uncool because that's the kind of thing that keeps folks from becoming too big for their britches. I've never met anyone who couldn't stand to eat a little bit of that humble pie, myself included.

THE STAFF MEETING FROM *Hell*

"Your hands really *are* all over the place. You need to work on keeping them at least below your face when you're talking."

Outwardly, I half nodded that I understood what they were saying. Internally, I screamed, "First of all, I don't remember asking y'all about my hands. And, second of all, yes, I know I'm too gesture-y when I talk, but I have no idea how to fix it without looking like a fucking T-Rex in a goddamn pantsuit and pearls."

Opinions are like belly buttons: everyone has one. In the case of a candidate's campaign staff, everyone has at least six. But being surrounded by people with a lot of opinions (and belly buttons) is better than being surrounded by sycophants. Smart, opinionated staffers who keep it real and honest with you make you a better candidate. If, for instance, during my campaign, I'd decided to 'dab' at the end of every public speaking event (because, you know, I'm young and hip), it would be extremely important that my staff tell me how stupid my idea is and physically stop me from dabbing in public. Smart leaders are surrounded by smart people telling them when they're doing or saying stupid shit.

Sitting around my dining room table, all six members of my newly formed campaign staff and I were going through our weekly updates. With the first candidate debate coming up, I was starting to feel some pressure. I hadn't participated in a debate since eighth grade (when I served as a kick-ass debate captain) and was beginning to mildly freak out over the possibility of embarrassing myself in front of a bunch of primary voters only a month into my campaign. I shifted the topic to debate prep. What should I wear? Probably not a skirt or dress in case I need to sit on a barstool or something, right?[4] Also, am I really supposed to pivot when I get a question I don't have an answer to? Isn't pivoting just a shameless and glaringly obvious attempt to ignore the question and instead answer a different question that nobody even asked in the first place? I don't like when politicians pivot, so can I just ... ... not do that?

Pivoting, my staff began answering questions I never even asked:

- "Why, yes, you ARE very gesture-y when you talk!"
- "Yeah, you're definitely an interrupter sometimes. Don't do that, okay?"
- "Yeah, your potty mouth will get you into trouble; make sure you don't accidentally let the F word slip!"
- "I'm not saying you're argumentative, I'm just saying that you like to argue with people."
- "Sometimes we can see what you're thinking because it's literally written all over your face. Definitely control your facial expressions when you're up there, okay?"
- "Also, don't exhale so exasperatedly when you're annoyed—people can totally tell."

Is it the norm for a bunch of people who *supposedly* like you and believe in you to so easily fire off a long-ass list of all your flaws and foibles? There I was, taking in all of this *new-to-me*

---

4 I have yet to master the perfect, Kate Middleton-esque ability to sit ladylike while in dresses and skirts in front of paparazzi.

information about myself while trying to do my best Patrick Bateman sociopath-who-feels-nothing impression. Obviously, I was totally playing it cool.

My entire body was overcome with an intense, hot rage. I pursed my lips and stopped blinking in an effort to assert dominance or something. The tension in my neck increased and radiated to my shoulders. My jaw clenched so tightly that I started to feel a migraine coming on. In the face of criticism, I was not graceful and poised. I was a snowflake with a headache.

I then did what any dignified leader would do in that situation: I made things hella awkward by letting emo-Silky have a few words.

"Jesus fucking Christ. Look, y'all. While these 'insights' (yes, I used air quotes …) are interesting, they're, you know, just your opinions, and I'll be taking them with a grain of salt. Mostly because I like the way I am even if it means I curse too much and I move my hands around like a crazy person. And besides, I'm not even THAT gesture-y, and I'm not argumentative at all. So slow your rolls, and please don't try and change me, okay?"

The silence that followed was so awkward that my dogs walked over from the living room to see why it had gotten so quiet. My staff sat looking at each other, but no one would make eye contact with me.

I still cringe when I think about how thin-skinned I was in that moment. My staff's constructive critiques had blindsided me. It was like I had popped into my supervisor's office to get a few pieces of fun-size Twix out of the bowl on their desk only for them to ask, "Would you sit down, please? I'd like to do your yearly performance review, but also, I'm going to be reviewing your performance in, you know, just life in general."

For the last couple of years, I've often wondered why that one meeting sticks out so much in my memory. I've realized it's because I felt stupid the whole time and am ashamed of how I lashed out at everyone for no real reason. Unsolicited criticism isn't fun, but shutting my whole staff down with a "Nuh uh, your FACE is argumentative" was as far away from displaying stoic, inspiring leadership as anyone could be. I wish I had come across as poised and possessing even the tiniest bit of grace. These staffers were there, after all, because they believed in me both as a person and as a candidate. They had been a bit south of tactful, maybe, but not unkind or malicious. I reacted like a child being scolded when I should have treated the whole thing as a chance at professional development. Had I been more lighthearted and jokey instead of overly sensitive, maybe everyone wouldn't have felt compelled to leave the meeting an hour early.

The moment I shined THE MOST was when my campaign manager suggested that I can, sometimes, ever so slightly, come across as argumentative when discussing highly-charged topics. I proceeded to argue with her loudly about why I am, in fact, NOT argumentative:

"Look. It's not arguing if I'm right! Okay?"

Checkmate, Silky.

THAT TIME I WON THE *Debate*

(Even Though There Were No Points or Scorekeeping, I Totally Won)

A pparently, paying a $3,000 filing fee to get on the ballot for United States Congress still doesn't guarantee people are going to take you or your candidacy seriously. There's this whole subjective criteria for how primary voters and politicos determine whether a candidate is deemed worthy of serious consideration. This was news to me. I actually didn't find out this was a thing until after I completely rocked it at the second primary debate.

Debates are hard. They're also boring when you're the one not talking. I would go from kind of zoned out to a full-on adrenaline rush whenever it was my turn to speak. Who needs illicit drugs when there are candidate debates to participate in?!

At the first debate in an election cycle, candidates don't really know the questions that will come up. Then, for each debate afterward, they hear the same damn questions over and over again, and they have to think of a million different, interesting ways to answer them.

The realization that I could be asked about anything in the known universe of politics had me in a full-on panic during my first debate prep. I felt like a freshman P.E. major preparing to take a graduate-level political science oral exam where literally anything covering the history of American politics and government could be on the test. Because this was all new to me, I really had no idea or game plan about how to prepare. I spent a week trying to learn everything about everything.

The week before, I attended a Democratic candidate debate for the congressional race in the district next to mine to get an idea of how our debate might go. I sat in the sprawling cafeteria

of a huge middle school watching all seven Democratic congressional candidates answer one question after the other on all
kinds of shit, from education to healthcare to military interven-
tion. I was kind of freaked out watching (mostly) all of them
speak to these issues with incredible depth and knowledge.
The candidates for that race included some lawyers, a doctor, a
Harvard Law grad, a former congressional staffer, and a woman
who was *literally* friends with the Obamas. Instead of helping
me feel prepared and confident for my own upcoming debate,
I left that cafeteria sure I was going to screw up and embarrass
myself only a few days later.

I didn't know what to expect. It was my first debate since
an eighth-grade UIL competition, and I completely kicked
ass at that one, helping my school come in second place. Why
wouldn't I be good now?

While I didn't suck during that first debate, I definitely stumbled and faltered much more than I anticipated I would. All
five candidates had to stand for over an hour, and as the only
candidate in heels, I lost, like, seventy-five percent of feeling in
my toes about halfway through the two-hour event and spent
the rest of the debate hyper-focused on shifting weight from
one foot to the other as subtly as humanly possible. I wasn't
the worst candidate, but I sure as hell felt like it at the time.
I was sweating profusely, but thank God I was wearing a black
blouse so no one could see the sweat line under my bra. Seated
at the very back was Lee, live-texting the play-by-play to the
rest of my team.

Watching the Facebook Live stream the next day in the kitchen while eating a cold Taco Bell bean burrito—extra onions, mild sauce, and cheese—had me cringing big time. I had this tiny fantasy that in my first public forum as a congressional candidate, I would come out of the gate swinging: wowing and dazzling all these voters, leaving them intoxicated with my young, fresh, progressive awesomeness, my clever quips about abortion rights and healthcare, and my blouse-with-bow, high-waisted wool trousers, and jet-black power high heels.

Instead, I was too hand gesture-y, rapidly and randomly switching between karate chopping my left hand with my right hand, thoughtfully pointing at the crowd with my Bill Clinton thumb, and turning both palms up like a spiritual leader, motioning toward the audience. Then, I was too non-hand-gesture-y, arms pinned to my sides as though I'd suddenly forgotten they were even there. I was less Michelle Obama and more Michael Flatley, Lord of the Dance.[5]

The room was also kind of small-ish and felt a bit cramped. Those of us who showed up early had to go from table to table asking the patrons seated in the main dining area of the Cafe Express if we could borrow their chairs for a political event happening in the back room, simultaneously inviting them to attend. Cue fifteen of us lugging forty of the heaviest, clunkiest chairs a fast casual dining establishment can offer and cramming them into a dimly lit room meant for a capacity of twenty-five. Space was so limited that one of the other

---

5   If you're under thirty, YouTube that shit. It's unreal.

candidates basically stood in front of me every time he had to answer a question, literally blocking my view of the audience. I wanted to be a baller, shot caller[6] that night, but I ended up average and mildly forgettable.

The second debate was set to take place one month later. It was being organized by several local Democratic Party clubs and orgs, so the crowd was anticipated to be several times larger than the first one. I was extra nervous, mostly because I felt like I had something to prove. Or rather, disprove. I know I'm not an average or forgettable person, and I wanted to make damn sure that by the end of the evening, everyone at that debate knew that I was in fact a baller, shot caller.

I had so much riding on this that I spent a decent amount of time preparing and practicing my stump speech, memorizing facts and figures (remember, I've got the memorization skills of a fruit fly[7]), and being appropriately hand gesture-y. I tried to put in the work to ensure my stage fright wouldn't stop me from saying the things that I needed to say to the audience.

My team and I—about ten of us—showed up around half an hour before the debate was set to start. I walked in and

---

6 This is a phrase made famous by Houston rapper Lil' Troy's 1998 hit, "Wannabe a Baller." In 1998, I was in eight grade, and this was the first rap song I had ever heard. The song's lyrics spoke to my soul, ensuring I'd spend the rest of my life earning the stately, distinguished title of "Baller, Shot Caller".

7 I'm assuming they're bad at memorizing things; Google didn't really yield any answers to this.

saw nearly two dozen people who looked like they had just walked out of an Abercrombie and Fitch catalogue circa 2001: tall, slim, gorgeous hair, great bone structure, and sunkissed tans (even though it was nearly winter), decked out in t-shirts emblazoned with the frontrunner's name, Todd Litton. Clearly, his staff had shown up WAY EARLIER than we had and were able to scope out the best spot to set up. Their campaign table (covered in a navy-blue tablecloth made of fabric nicer than the ones used for my own wedding) was super swagged out, full-on flush with clicky pens (the good quality ones, too), buttons AND stickers, tons of extra tees, stacks on stacks of *full-color* printouts with all kinds of important information for voters, clipboards as far as the eye could see, and complete with the pièce de résistance: a freakin' tabletop easel with a child-sized foam board map of the district! They even had their yard signs ready to go.

Our table setup was kinda sad by comparison: a long, white plastic Costco folding table (sans tablecloth), barely fit to sell Girl Scout cookies off of, adorned with only a *few* clipboards, regular, boring, non-Silky-labeled non-clicky pens, a sign with my campaign logo on it (more the size of an overweight Pomeranian than a child), and zero buttons or yard signs because they weren't ready yet. Adding insult to injury, literally NONE of us on my team looked even a tiny bit like an Abercrombie & Fitch model (except, of course, Imran).

I don't think I've ever felt so small potatoes in my life. In that moment, walking into this huge union hall and seeing my opponent's swagalicious table, the sheer magnitude of what

I was attempting to do suddenly dawned on me. I was such a noob. I suddenly felt SO young and instantly became hyper-aware of the fact that I was the only woman in this race, and that I was a literal nobody who was obviously cosplaying an adult running for U.S. Congress.

On the other hand, this dude, Todd Litton, had clearly spent a large part of his life planning his congressional run. From his booming voice to his navy blazer, straight down to his khaki pants, he walked, talked, and looked the part of a U.S. Congressman. He even had the right amount of salt and pepper in his hair, making him look more distinguished than old. He had all the bona fides to prove he was ready for Capitol Hill: impressive private university for undergrad, a degree from a law school deep in the heart of Texas, and nonprofit work that intersected perfectly with his vast network of important and influential friends.

Meanwhile, I'm over here with my way-too-long-for-politics hair and a shift dress that suddenly felt too snug around my curvy hips and a tad too short to pass for business professional when I sat down. I had, like, no bona fides at all—an amateur amongst these other "serious" guys.

I had known for all of a year that I was going to run for Congress, and for some reason, I felt like that was a strike against me as a candidate. At the very beginning of my run, I had this weird notion that because I hadn't spent my whole life gearing up to run for Congress, people wouldn't think I was legit. In some ways, this was true; my reasons for running weren't particularly professional or ambitious or, for that matter, even well-planned. Nope. I was a Johnny-come-lately to politics, running for the sole purpose of answering a moral imperative.

When I saw how underprepared we were when it came to something as simple as swagging out a campaign table, I really, for a hot minute, felt convinced that my debate performance would be just as sad and un-baller, un-shot caller as our table was. A wave of pre-pubescent insecurity washed over me. I was certain I wasn't good enough to be there doing this very big, very grown-up, very serious thing. At that moment, I so desperately wished I had the typical political pedigree and resume; I chastised myself for having studied psychology and sociology as an undergrad and not becoming a lawyer. *God Silky. Why on earth did you want to be a researcher?!* Everything about my candidacy suddenly felt random and dumb, and I wished I had just stayed in my lane and not attempted to shoehorn myself into someplace I didn't belong. I've spent a lot of my life being the odd duck out, but the sudden feeling of being a lame interloper was entirely new to me.

I gave serious thought to doing whatever the political equivalent of *bride sneaks out of the bathroom window to avoid saying "I do"* is. Maybe I'd pack up my three clipboards, two folding stools, and stack of candidate information cards, slip out the back, and drive home. Or had we brought a damn tablecloth for our table I could've just hidden under there to wait it out.

Thankfully, talking to people is my Xanax, and as soon as a voter came up and asked me a question, I forgot that I was supposed to be Irish goodbye-ing this gig. Also, there were too many people there that evening for me to flake on the entire debate without being noticed. Also, as usual, Imran made me stay.

The debate went by in a blur at breakneck speed. When asked about abortion rights, I quipped, "I knew I was a feminist when I learned about Roe v. Wade in middle school" and got a big laugh from the audience (yeah, yeah, the bar for funny is low in politics, I know). Suddenly, all of my nervousness just vanished. I felt electrified. I *knew* I was in it to win it. I got a huge applause from the room after nearly every response I gave.

Early on in my campaign, probably before I even announced that I was running, I decided to be as honest, candid, and plainspoken as I could be. I wasn't going to waste folks' time being wishy-washy or hesitant and overly measured when answering their questions. No one wants to talk to a robot who spits out canned responses. That shit is both boring and infuriating. I was going to make my life on the trail easy and uncomplicated by keeping all of my responses simple and direct. *Keep it real, yo*, was my campaign motto.[8]

Every time I was asked a question during the debate, I answered it like I was talking to a group of my friends or family (minus the cursing, of course!). In stark contrast to nearly all the other candidates, I did not bullshit my fellow Houstonians even once when giving an answer.

Moderator: Candidates, what are your thoughts on the legalization of marijuana?

---

8 This was also the motto for how to be your flyest self in the mid-nineties.

Robot Candidate: Great question! It's important that we look at this issue and study it from the lens of how we can best make policy that is both good and effective for all Americans. I'm excited to bring this can-do spirit of good and effective change to Washington.

Silky: Look, y'all. We ALL know that weed's been legal for white kids for at least twenty years. We need to stop using the "War on Drugs" as an excuse to disproportionately arrest Black and Brown kids, so let's instead legalize weed and tax the hell out of it.

With each response I gave, I got confirmation from the crowd that I was on a freaking roll.

To this day, I know for a fact that I walked into that union hall an unknown entity and walked out a candidate to be taken seriously.

There's that word again. "Serious." Ugh. Politics is always so "serious," and if you're not "serious enough" (whatever that means), no one will take your candidacy "seriously." I didn't think that I was or wasn't coming across as "serious." I'm not even sure how to be "serious," y'all. All I know how to do is be myself, maybe cuss a little less than usual, be confident in what I know, and be eager to learn about the things I don't know.

And yet, after the debate, person after person came up to me and my husband and gushed about how great I was and how nice it was to see that I was a "serious" candidate.

Ummm. Okay, then. Thanks?

You gotta love politics. Even on a great night when you're awesome, you're still going to be showered with backhanded compliments.

THE
#SilkySquad

My name is pretty weird. For as long as I can remember, I've only ever had two cool nicknames.

In ninth grade, a few kids intermittently called me Silky Smooth. I tried so hard to make it stick because I thought it would make me sound cool and smooth, like an R&B starlette. But nope. I couldn't, like, *get* anyone to use this nickname of their own will and volition. This was a nickname that was, and still is, used pretty sporadically.

Nearly twenty years later, at my first real job post-college, a co-worker, Erin, left a Post-it note on my monitor that said, "Silky Pants! Come find me. We need to talk!" I worked in a shared office, so several other people had seen Erin's note and clearly liked the new moniker enough that the whole research team started calling me Silky Pants by the time lunch rolled around. It is my favorite nickname to date and holds a special place in my heart. Thank you forever, Erin. <3

Other nicknames I have had which are not cool:

Silky Worm

While reading *James and the Giant Peach* aloud to the class, my fourth-grade teacher, Mrs. Stoller, accidentally called the character Silkworm, Silky Worm.

Silk Stockings

In fifth grade, a fellow student, Lauren, who was evidently allowed to watch cable TV without parental supervision, told a group of us walking home together after school how great the

TV show *Silk "Stalkings"* was. This was hilarious to everyone, even me, until I learned that "stockings" was actually another word for pantyhose. I immediately hated my parents for making me a latchkey kid who walked home instead of those other, *loved* kids whose parents could pick them up from school, in a car, safe from the lingerie-inspired nicknames awaiting them on the walk home.

Silky Drawls

My fifth-grade elementary school principal was a kind, affable man who always did his best to engage students and make us laugh. He was also a "cool adult," and upon learning my name, belted, "Silky? Like Silky Drawls!" This was in the cafeteria, now the birthplace of one of the stickier nicknames I'd been given up to that point. I wouldn't shed this nickname for at least three years, until I switched neighborhoods and my new school didn't have any kids from my old school.

Silky Cotton Polyester

For some reason still inexplicable to me, this was a popular nickname from eighth grade to about tenth grade, that only the boys who were in athletics seemed to call me. They thought it was hilarious. I'm still kinda neutral on it.

Sophie

In eleventh-grade bio class, Karla accidentally called me Sophie. For some reason, that one stuck until I graduated.

At least once a year since I was in high school, someone I've just met, upon hearing my name, will remark "Ha! That's like a stripper's name!" This also happened to me when I was fifteen and called into the radio station to request a song, and DJ Captain Obvious informed all of Houston, "Ha! Silky?! That's a stripper's name!"

When I decided to run for office, I immediately knew I would use my first name on my campaign materials: Silky for Congress. I liked it. It felt very authentic. I also feel so much more connected to my first name than I ever have to my last name, both maiden and married.

There were quite a few folks who expressed judgment at my "branding" choice and claimed I was being purposefully vague about my race, gender, and religious affiliation. I was misleading the voters by obfuscating the Hindu and Muslim origins of my name, my *identity*! By only using my first name, how would voters know who I *am*? They wouldn't know *who* or *what* they were voting for. How *unethical*!

Even "good Democrats" can dog whistle, whether or not they mean to.

I have spent most of my life leaning into the weirdness of my name.

"Haha, yeah. It *is* a unique name. What can I say, the eighties were wild!"

I refused to shy away from the oddness or foreign-ness of my name or who I am. And, much to my surprise, the voters I met on the trail were pretty neutral or neutral-positive about potentially voting for the Indian girl with a weird name to be their next congresswoman.

Even more surprising was the first time someone said they wanted to join the "Silky Squad" and volunteer for the campaign. It had only taken thirty-four years, but I was finally cool enough to be the leader of a squad! Obviously, this being the age of social media, we printed that baby onto t-shirts and encouraged folks to use #SilkySquad every chance they got.

During my run in 2017, I was one of the only candidates in my area who used their first name as the primary moniker for their campaign.[9] It was a constant source of comments and questions, mainly because, at the time, it was a little unusual. This year, though, in my (very large) county, I can count at least five candidates who are using their first name out on the campaign trail. Several of these candidates also have unique or non-American sounding first and last names, so it feels kind of amazing to see the way folks are making a place for themselves in a space that's been pretty homogenous until now.

---

9   Well, me and Beto (O'Rourke)—clearly, I keep good company. 2018 Senate hopeful, 2020 presidential candidate, and all around Political Bae, Beto O'Rourke took the nation by storm with his senatorial campaign for a reason. A punk rock skateboarder who loved Whataburger, played concerts with Willie Nelson, and dropped the occasional F-bomb, he showed the country that Texas was ready for a new brand of politics and a new breed of politician.

YOU SUCK
AND HERE'S
THE PROOF:
Endorsements

"**O**kay, so hear me out. I'm not going tomorrow. I think I'm just gonna call in sick."

Campaign manager: Um. That's not a … *thing*. You can't call in sick to an endorsement screening with the biggest newspaper in Texas. You either go tomorrow, or you don't get to screen.

Me, channeling my thirteen-year-old self, theatrically sprawled out on the living room floor: This suuuucks! I've been rejected, like, ten times now by every place I've screened with. UGH. It's not like I'm going to get it anyway.

I was trying in vain to convince my campaign manager how it would be *totally* fine for me to bail on my endorsement screening with the Houston Chronicle, Texas's most-read newspaper. I had just come off of two straight weeks of grueling endorsement screenings without having secured a single one. The conversation ended with me petulantly reminding my campaign manager that I was a GROWN UP and they couldn't *make* me do something I didn't feel like doing! I hung up the phone knowing full well that I was going to show up to the damn screening whether I felt like it or not.

I was on day four of possibly the worst migraine of my life. The intense throbbing anytime I blinked or tried to speak had me fairly convinced I was dying. While I acknowledged how embarrassing it would be to die less than a month before my primary election, I realized maybe dying wouldn't be so bad. If I dropped dead in the waiting area of the Chron, surely that would garner me a positive mention in their endorsement! All publicity is good publicity, right?

I really hadn't heard much about endorsement screenings prior to running for office. I can sort of vaguely recall coming across the Houston Chronicle's endorsement of then-Senator Barack Obama for his presidential campaign in 2008, but until 2017, I had no earthly idea how endorsements even worked.

I first learned about endorsements when perusing my opponents' campaign websites. The frontrunner's website boasted a very long list of endorsements, and watching that list grow daily was both annoying and intimidating. But I wasn't too worried because I thought I would be great at endorsement screenings. I always fancied myself pretty good at interviews; I'm witty, chatty, charming—and dare I say it—kinda popular! Who *wouldn't* love me?! I'd have these endorsement panels eating out of the palm of my hand! Winning an endorsement was gonna be as easy as showing up in a baller outfit, flashing my pearly whites, and firing off a few finger guns (*pew pew!*) before waltzing out with my well-deserved trophy.

Turns out the sole job of the endorsement panel is to make you question how you ever managed to make it to the age of thirty-four oblivious to how truly unlovable and unlikable you really are. Seriously. I'll be damned if I didn't feel like a comedian whose each and every joke fell flat, eliciting groans and the occasional boo from a not-nearly-drunk-enough audience. Whatever the opposite of "you like me, you really like me!" is —that's what I felt during and after each of these screenings. Tough crowd would be an understatement.

Here's how it works:

Within a few weeks of officially filing with the state to run for office, various organizations, groups, and clubs send out an email inviting the candidate to screen with them in an attempt to earn their endorsement. An endorsement often includes awesome, tangible things like block walking, phone banking, hosting meet and greets, and sending out mailers on your behalf. It isn't just some feel-good, fluffy accolade; this boots-on-the-ground help can make or break a candidate's campaign. Not too shabby … if you can get it.

Once the endorsement paperwork[10] is filled out, the candidate is invited to interview. If you're a first-time candidate like I was, you may be thinking, "Hey, why do I need to screen with the GLBT Caucus or Black Democrats or Teacher's Union? I'm literally a gay, Black, dues-paying teacher's union member!" Well, belonging to a group won't automatically earn you their endorsement. Not seeking out an endorsement is basically a big FU to the org and will prompt members of the political or activist community to assume your campaign is not interested in or concerned about the issues facing the communities these organizations represent. So, yeah, you definitely cannot opt out. However, you should definitely ignore endorsement screening requests from organizations that don't align with your political/ moral beliefs. For instance, I declined to fill out anything from groups like the NRA, anti-LGBTQ pastors' associations, the

---

10   By the way, these questionnaires can be SUPER long. Like, midterm paper long. A few of them required extensive research and essay writing!

charter school lobby, etc. So feel free to delete emails from the Murder All Puppies Political Action Committee.

Meanwhile, even if you're convinced everyone hates you and you are throwing yourself a one-woman pity party, you probably shouldn't bail on your endorsement screening with the city's major newspaper.

My interview with the Houston Chronicle was the last one before the March primary election. It was also, in many ways, the most important endorsement I could get. Some candidates have practically won their entire election thanks to an endorsement from the Chronicle.

Up until that point, I had screened with the Houston GLBT Political Caucus, the Harris County Tejano Democrats, the Harris County AFL-CIO, the Airline Pilots Association, Harris County's chapter of Our Revolution, Houston's chapter of Democratic Socialists of America, and, like, a million other groups across the City of Houston.

What frustrated me the most about getting rejected over and over again was hearing afterward how much the panel liked me and my take on the issues affecting the groups they represented, but unfortunately, I was unelectable because I hadn't raised enough money or because I was too young and new to politics to jump straight into a race for federal office. That I wasn't *viable*. One screener even had the gall to suggest I should have run for something more appropriate for my age and experience, like school board, perhaps.

Walking into the Houston Chronicle screening with a grand total of zero endorsements under my belt, I felt like a total nobody loser no one liked enough to support. Add to this the worst migraine of my life, and it was all I could do to even show up.

Interview-mode Silky is extra bubbly, witty, and effusive. Houston-Chronicle-endorsement-screening Silky was not any of those things. In fact, I was in so much pain from the migraine and so OVER being rejected and feeling like a loser that I was probably the least chatty, most direct, and most serious version of myself that I had ever been. I knew I wasn't going to secure the endorsement, so I was determined to be as succinct as possible with my responses in the desperate hope of getting it over with so I could go home and lie down. For the first time in my professional life, and during an interview no less, I was physically unable to break the ice with jokes or fill awkward silences with mindless chatter. Every time I spoke, my skull filled with the bonging and banging of a million brass bells being rung at once. So completely on accident, and thanks to the migraine from hell, I'm pretty sure I came off as some sort of Xena: Warrior Princess badass. Which, I totally am, like, in my soul. But on the outside, most of the time, I don't come across nearly as serious or as fierce as I did that day.

When the Chronicle printed their endorsement recommendations, I saw Todd's big ol' pic and felt lame all over again. Initially, I didn't even bother to read past the first paragraph. As the day wore on, though, my phone chimed nonstop with texts from people congratulating me on the flattering write-up the Chron had included about me (and no other candidate) in their endorsement of Todd.

Printed on February 19, 2018:

> Also impressive is Silky Malik, 34, a self-styled millennial candidate with a deep earnestness about her generation's desire for honest, straightforward politicians who will work to improve the material conditions of the middle class in the model of President Franklin D. Roosevelt …

> 'It feels almost out of date to think that our government can do things for this country that aren't self-serving,' Malik said.

I still hadn't gotten any endorsements, but the biggest newspaper in my home state had given me one hell of a shout-out, and I was gonna ride that high all the way to Election Day.

CYNICAL AND *Elected*

Midday luncheons are sort of a new occurrence in my life.[11] Prior to my participation in politics, I had never really been to one. But, apparently, these luncheons happen ALL THE TIME. There's probably one going on right now as I'm writing this:

- The Luncheon for Lefty Liberals (inexplicably for Bloomberg for President)
- The Asians for American Academics (a.k.a. the Asians Against Affirmative Action because we believe it helps Black kids more than Asian kids) Get Woke Gala
- The Moms Against School Shootings (unless the school is in the poor part of town) Luncheon

At first, I used to really look forward to these events. Getting dressed up extra nice (thank you, Rent The Runway!) and going to a fancy hotel ballroom downtown was so fun and new to me even though once I got there, I felt awkward and out of place.[12] Even now, when I go somewhere marginally fancier than Taco Bell, I still kind of feel that way, but as soon as I see a familiar face, the awkwardness disappears and I'm just left feeling out of place. Regardless, there's always a fair amount of pomp and circumstance at these political shindigs, and I totally eat that shit up and generally enjoy myself a ton.

Usually these luncheons have a really good speaker. Last year, I saw Stacey Abrams speak at the Annie's List luncheon,

---

11 Well, they were two and a half years ago. Now they're old hat. Oh man. I sound like a monocle-wearing, top-hat-adorned member of the liberal elite, don't I?!

12 A Little Awkward and Out of Place, the title of my second book.

fresh off of having the Georgia Governor's seat stolen from her via election fraud and voter suppression. Speaking to a room packed with my fellow Houstonians, she reminded us that "We have the power to fight back." I leave these events ready to kick ass and take names, full of hope and inspiration that we *can* be the change we want to see. Very hippie-dippie and kumbaya, I know, but I'm a sucker for feel-good sappiness, so, again, I eat that shit up.

But even if the speaker is inspiring and the cause worthwhile, one of your tablemates will undoubtedly leave a lot to be desired. Though ninety percent of folks in attendance are of the earnest, endlessly kind, bleeding-heart variety, chances are you'll be sharing your table with one of the following:

The Shameless Self-Promoter

This person is either rich and kinda (locally) famous or *wants* to be rich and kinda (locally) famous. Expect tons of selfies and blank stares in response to any question you may ask. Despite any effort you put forward to engage them in conversation, the Shameless Self-Promoter will constantly leave their seat to find someone better or more important to talk to.

The Nonstop Talker

Bless their heart, but Lord have mercy, please let me hear what the speaker is saying! I don't care if you think the chicken is dry. I don't care if you came in fourth in the primary for the school board in 1992. I don't even know you. Please, just text your running commentary to a friend or something.

The Social Butterfly

They know *so many people* at this event that they absolutely *have* to get up during *every* four-minute break to flit from table to table, saying a quick hello to all their friends. The Social Butterfly is annoying because instead of being present and chatting up their tablemates, they're up and out of their seat as soon as it's appropriate to do so.

This person is me. I'm the worst, I know. I wasn't always *like this*, y'all! But after almost three years of being part of my local activist/political community, I have tons of friends, and we often only get to see one another at stuff like this. Plus, my tablemate won't freaking stop talking about how dry the chicken is and a race they ran in before I was even BORN.

The Wannabe Elected

The mutant child of the Shameless Self-Promoter and the Social Butterfly, this person arrives late or leaves obnoxiously early because they've got somewhere else to be. They're pretty thirsty to grab a photo with any important people in attendance, and they're gonna get **pissed** if they aren't allowed to take a picture with Nancy Pelosi.

You don't always know or like the folks you're seated next to at one of these things. Typically, though, you can assume that if they've spent the money to sit through a meal of dry chicken and watered-down iced tea, they're a progressive who's down for the cause. Even though the Shameless Self-Promoter, the Nonstop Talker, the Social Butterfly, and the Wannabe Elected can be kinda annoying, they're still usually good people. Despite some social quirks, we're all trying to make the world a little bit better.

But, there's one type of tablemate whose toxic worldview is a goddamn bummer:

The Cynical Elected

The Cynical Elected believes in democracy, but they don't believe in people.

I'm starting to realize that I've spent a lot of my life (wrongly) believing that people who share at least one of the same labels as me—woman, Indian, minority, child of immigrants, Democrat, progressive, etc.—must also share my values. Chalk it up to youthful naivete (yes, thirty-six is considered youthful) that has clearly stuck around for too long. My naivete is probably the reason why I'm often shocked or disappointed when a label-mate says something batshit, obnoxious, or out of touch.

I remember one luncheon in particular that highlighted interesting and accomplished women in Houston and gave attendees an opportunity to learn how these trailblazers were currently making history. An event with all-women speakers is totally my jam, so I was definitely living my best, nerdiest life that afternoon. Well, I was until I got some not-so-helpful insight from the Cynical Elected seated at my table.

Sometime after we'd finished eating lunch and listening to our last speaker, I tried striking up a conversation. I asked about her work and how she found her way into politics. Soon after, another woman from my table joined our conversation, and we began discussing corruption in politics. Ooh! Yes!! Here I was, in a room full of brilliant and highly accomplished women, and this conversation was about to get intellectual and hella deep. Except it wasn't. The only "knowledge bomb" the Cynical Elected dropped that day was the notion that poor people shouldn't run for office.

"Look, all I'm saying is if someone wanted to 'buy me off' or bribe me or whatever, they'd have to offer me, like, fifty-million dollars or something. Which most people don't really have the money to do, right? It's much harder to bribe someone when the price is that high and especially if they don't need the money."

Um, what now? Did this person literally just imply that poor people are more easily corruptible because they need the money?

This Cynical Elected was a well-liked, dyed-in-the-wool Democrat, and yet, whether she intended to or not, had said poor people couldn't really ever become trustworthy elected officials.

Leaning forward, I thought to ask for clarification, to call her out for the blatantly classist dog whistle we'd all just heard. Instead, I hesitated, and she sauntered off to greet someone else before I could say a single word.

That afternoon, I walked out of the ballroom with a weird sinking feeling in my stomach. Instead of giving the Cynical Elected the verbal middle finger, I had stood there mute. I was so disappointed in myself for being unable to speak up in the moment. But it was more than just that. For the first time in my life, I was accidentally made privy to the way wealthy and establishment politicians—both Republicans and Democrats—view the other ninety-nine percent of Americans:

As people who are not fit to lead or have a seat at the table because we aren't pedigreed enough.

At thirty-six, I am more financially secure and comfortable than I ever thought I would be.

My life is *very* privileged.

The first time I ever felt this newfound privilege was when I filled my gas tank all the way up without having to check my account balance before pulling into the station. In a few more years, I will have spent a longer time being well-off than I have spent being poor and broke. Ironically, this fills me with uneasiness and fear that someday I'll forget where I came from, only to end up hanging out with a bunch of Monopoly-looking mofos, wearing monocles, smoking fat cigars, top hats askew just so, twirling our handlebar mustaches, delighting in the latest corporate tax cut that fucked over hundreds of millions of Americans.

Since running for office, I now spend weirdly large amounts of time hanging in the vicinity of the kind of people we created the phrase "generational wealth" for, and who actually know why Mitch McConnell wants to abolish the Estate Tax. Folks who vote Democrat but are vocally scared of politicians like Bernie Sanders, Elizabeth Warren, and AOC.

Oftentimes, I am one of a small handful of "poor kids" at a gathering of these fancy folk. I used to be outside the tent pissing in, but nowadays, I'm sort of just pissing in the tent, which is as messy and strange a line to walk as it sounds.

Although politics and activism can benefit from the support of well-heeled liberals, I refuse to pretend the top one percent aren't the ones fucking up the world. So when Richie Rich starts fear-mongering at a dinner party about how SoCiALiSm(!!!), free college education, universal healthcare, and a living mini-mum wage are destroying this country while I'm standing there in my beautiful, bought-at-retail-price silk dress with my hair professionally blown out, wearing vintage diamond earrings (worth more than my first car) gifted to me for Christmas by my mother-in-law, I talk about my reliance on the need-based education loans and government healthcare that got me into the same tax bracket that he's in.

I think and talk about my upbringing a lot. So much of who I am today and the moral compass that guides my life is due to the struggles, hardships, and financial adversity I experienced growing up, and I don't want to ever distance myself from that.

I'm standing here inside this political tent, pissing everywhere (how's that for some great mental imagery?) because I want our government to be better. If I kept quiet or laughed along anytime some rich liberal screeched about dEmOcRaTiC sOcIaLiSm (!!!), I'd be perpetuating a system of classism that makes it so hard for regular people to get elected.

Sure, it might be less awkward if I didn't pepper my conversations with poor-kid anecdotes every time I was at a political shindig, but I do it because I don't want to forget who I am, or where I came from, à la "Jenny from the Block."

Campaigning at the Women's March. Cynthia, Sarah, Kenny, Me, Jeffrey, Courtney

#SilkySquad
#T-ShirtSwag

Candidates coming together for Democracy! HP, Todd, Me, Ali

First volunteer shift ever!

Friends who show up to help when you didn't ask is the best feeling ever!

Left: Elenita at the polls. *Right:* Wes at the polls!

That face you make when you're so exhausted you could cry, but you smile anyway for a selfie with your friend Bill. Also, thank God for the friends I made on the trail getting me through the more tiring parts of campaigning.

#SilkySquad #FamilySquad
Imran, Sana, and Omer

This is my "OMG I'm famous!!!"
face. Also, happy bday to Josh!

My brother Shane, doing up-close magic for
an intrigued Francesco at my campaign kickoff

Sana, Me, and my Mom
#FamilyForLife #FreeLabor

Picture proof I don't always
embarrass my mom

Our first candidate debate…in the back of a Café Express

POLITICS
IS WEIRD,
AND SO ARE
THE *People*

The world of politics is a microcosm of the world at large. In politics—at least Democratic politics—I get to meet people from literally all walks of life, and I've found this to be the absolute best side effect of throwing myself into this wacky world. From quirky to wholesome to nefarious, people in politics really are the IRL version of the joke "a priest, a rabbi, and a cowboy walk into a bar …"

Here are just a few of the folks you'll meet out on the trail.

The Saboteur

During my campaign kickoff party, I met a lovely girl who had "heard about your campaign and wanted to check it out!!!!!!" We even took a couple of pictures together! Turns out, she was an intern for one of my opponents and had been sent to scope out how much of a threat I was.

The Saboteur isn't always as benign as the girl sent to spy on me at my kickoff. A friend of mine who ran for the state legislature in a neighboring state told me about staff she had hired who would constantly do things wrong or mess up, seemingly on purpose. Every week, an email would go out wrong, or not even go out at all. Volunteers would be sent to events late or to the wrong location. Only when the internal discord and chaos rendered her staff unable to work together and caused people to quit in droves did she realize this employee wasn't just incompetent but was actively working to sabotage her campaign. With a near skeleton staff in place leading up to November's midterms, she ended up losing.

▶ **Moral of the story:** Vet your staff and any newcomers to your inner circle as well as you can!

The Politico

Ugh. This person sucks and doesn't seem to really believe in the power of the People. The Politico has likely never run for office themselves, but is "totally planning on it someday when all my ducks are in a row."

Despite never having had the guts to run for office, they sure do seem to fancy themselves political experts of the highest degree. They strut around like political oracles who are benevolent enough to shower you with tons of unsolicited insight and advice into the political process. They'll tell you you're wasting your time because you're not [insert boring, unoriginal, D.C.-establishment suggestion] enough.

Examples of annoying advice from the Politico include but are not limited to:

- Volunteer on [insert random number] of campaigns so you can be taken "seriously" as a candidate.

- Run for school board before you run for a "higher" or "more important" office.

- Don't go to events or attend gatherings where there isn't a chance to speak or ask someone for money. Caring about your community doesn't pay the campaign bills, so stop being involved or social for free! See also: don't spend more than twenty seconds talking to scrubby normies who can't max out their donations to you.

- Don't take your spouse with you to events because, as a woman, it's just going to make you look weak.

- Maybe cut your hair; seems kinda long since you're running for Congress, no?
- Don't say "y'all" all the time. Sounds too folksy.

Often, they're the "both sides are the same" dude who proclaims to have *totally* predicted Trump's victory "literally, from the moment he announced." They're the person who tells you not to run for office because "you're sort of a nobody who won't be able to fundraise, so you might as well not waste your time."

The worst Politico is the guy who literally knows "every important person in D.C." on a first-name basis and is full of helpful advice on how to "bring D.C. to Texas." This yahoo will criticize your grassroots efforts as being "not money focused" and doomed for failure because you're out block walking and holding town halls instead of being on the phone asking for money 24/7. They truly believe that there's only one type of campaign to run, and it's the kind cooked up by the Democratic Congressional Campaign Committee (D-Triple-C). The Politico wants a centrist candidate who spends all of their time with high net worth donors and politicos and won't rock the boat. Blah.

If you're anything but a total political insider running for office, the Politico thinks you're a joke with your head in the clouds, pushing for change that "America isn't ready for." They call themselves a Liberal and Progressive, but too much of the shit that comes out of their mouth is Republican Lite at best and, at worst, soul-crushingly uninspiring. This person will constantly encourage you to go against your gut on who you should be as a candidate. My recommendation is to smile at them politely while ignoring every stupid word that comes out of their mouth.

▶ **Moral of the story:** Fuck the establishment, y'all.

The Know-It-All

Oof. This person is sort of like the 'Politico' without all the negativity and unsolicited advice. They regard themselves as an academic and subject-matter expert on what truly makes a politician "electable." It's, like, ALL THEY TALK ABOUT. "eLeCtAbiLitY mAtTeRs!!!!" they scream at their friends, their family on Thanksgiving, and whoever else will listen. Reddit is a cesspool of these people who get themselves worked up and go yell at strangers on Facebook. They might also moonlight as a consultant, similar to the Politico, but because they're fancier and, like, worked as a congressional staffer after college or some shit twenty-five years ago, they charge a lot for their cookie-cutter consultancy playbook. Because they *apparently* know *everyone* who's *anyone* in D.C. (did you know that they've met both Obama AND Bush!?), they know who is and isn't electable—it's basically like a science for them.

▶ **Moral of the story:** Ignore this trifling-ass dude or dudette.

The Non-Voting Libertarian

Not to be confused with the non-voter who, upon asking some good-faith questions, is likely to register to vote right there on the spot, and pinky promises to vote in the primary, the Non-Voting Libertarian doesn't really believe we live in a democracy. We're all just peons being controlled by the Man, and there's nothing we can do to change or fix it because the whole system is rigged, so why even vote, dude? Also, if you're extra unlucky that day, they'll throw in a few Q-Anon and Deep State references.

Please learn from my mistake and do not talk to this person for more than ten minutes, because if you do, it will devolve into what can only be described as Twitter-arguing with Russian bots, but in actual real life: "Look, bro, I'm not saying that Trump is a great president, I'm just saying that Hillary was crooked, she murdered a lot of people through her Clinton Foundation, AND she didn't go to Wisconsin!!!! See. That's why I don't even vote." But if they ever have voted in the past, it was for Republicans because "taxation is theft."

This person will suck you into an hour of bad-faith arguments on why "bOtH sIdEs ArE tHe SaMe!11!" and "this is why Trump won and is gonna win again."

▶ **Moral of the story:** You cannot change the Non-Voting Libertarian's entire worldview, especially not in five minutes in the middle of a meet and greet at a bar, so just nod politely, shake their hand, and walk away fast, bro.

The Mean Girl

"Oh … Um. Wow. *You're* running for office? Why … ?"

There will be no "congratulations!" or "that's awesome, girl!!" or "how can I help?!" Nope. Instead, you'll get a look of confusion and a bewildered "when did you even *decide* this? Because you know Joe Schmoe, your Democratic primary opponent, has basically been planning to run for *years.*"

This chick seems to be weirdly upset that you're running for office *instead* of her because, after all, she *did* study government at [insert prestigious Ivy League university] and was *totally* going to run for something in a few years.

The mean girl and her friends, who you kinda thought you were cool with since you run in some of the same social justice/activism circles, will probably ghost you, and definitely won't volunteer or donate to your campaign. They LOVE posting on Insta about "women helping women," but they will definitely overlook the hypocrisy of not helping the only woman in the race.

▶ **Moral of the story:** It's not you, it's them. Don't take it personally.

The True Believer

This wonderful carbon copy of Leslie Knope is literally the reason you'll find the will to keep going during some of the worst moments of your campaign. They believe in you and your platform so completely that you'll find yourself borrowing from their never-ending pool of energy and optimism when you're too exhausted to muster up any fucks to give. Thank God for these amazing souls doing the work of democracy with a smile on their face and pep in their step.

▶ **Moral of the story:** Keep the true believers close and let their optimism rub off on you.

The Stan (Yes, like the Eminem song ft. Dido)

At first, the Stan might seem like a True Believer, except they're, like, obsessed with you. They could be someone who stalks your Facebook, Twitter, and Instagram and is constantly posting weird-ass comments even if you've never met IRL. Or, like in my case, the Stan was a volunteer who complained several times over the course of a single week via email that I "didn't ever hug him" when I greeted him and "neither do any of the other female volunteers/staff."

Needless to say, I was beyond furious that some random person felt entitled to any level of physical affection from me or my staff and was threatening me over email for a week. As a Texan with a Republican father who raised me on country music and movies starring Charles Bronson and Clint Eastwood, my first instinct was to tell him to "fuck off," then go to Academy and buy a handgun. I got as far as putting the gun on hold and leaving to run back home for my driver's license before my husband intervened and talked me off the ledge. Fortunately, Imran and Lee had a conversation with the Stan, "fired" him from our volunteer team, and I never had to go all Annie Oakley on his ass. So, yeah, putting yourself in the public eye means the weirdos are gonna come out the woodwork.

▶ **Moral of the story:** Worry less about being nice than doing whatever you can to make sure you feel safe. Just because you want to be a public servant doesn't mean you're giving up your right to privacy, respect, or safety.

The Convert

The Convert spent much of their life not really caring about politics, or if they did, they were hardcore conservatives or Republicans. They voted only sporadically, or just during the presidential races, but now they're voting in municipal elections and midterms and are totally "Vote Blue No Matter Who." These people are the reason folks like me (and you!) should continue running for office at every level—because we're able to grow the electorate by engaging non-voters and new voters in ways that haven't happened before.

I really loved meeting these folks on the trail. Because they haven't been through the emotional ringer of following politics for most of their life, they've got a lot of energy and optimism. They're not as burned out as some of the seasoned politicos, so they're ready to throw you house parties filled with neighbors they may not know very well. The Convert is ready and willing to do new things in their community, even if doing so makes them a little bit nervous.

My absolute favorite memory is of someone asking me how they can print their ballot and fill it out before going to the polls. They then decided to text all their friends and family about who they were voting for in the primary and offered to email their ballot to everyone. Someone who had never voted in a primary before, the Convert was now overcoming the self-described awkwardness of broaching politics with their friends and family to get out the vote.

▶ **Moral of the story:** These people are the reason you're running for office. Democracy persists one Convert at a time.

The Ghosts

These are your friends, family members, co-workers, and acquaintances who find politics so uncomfortable that no amount of love and respect for you will draw them into your campaign. These folks are probably cool with doing their civic duty every year but being around anything *politics* makes their skin crawl, and they'll basically disappear until your election is over. They just want to live their life, man. Go to work, pick the kids up from school, maybe get a few CrossFit workouts in this week, and watch the game on Sunday.

Try not to hold it against them. Until I ran, I never realized just how many people are really and truly icked out by just the *idea* of politics or politicians being in their orbit.

▶ **Moral of the story:** They'll come back around when things settle down and you're their "normal" friend again. Unless you win. In that case, I have no idea what the hell happens to these people! If I ever find out, I'll be sure to update you in my second book.

The Gatekeepers

Some folks grew up connected to the political world. They have uncles who were senators in the eighties, grandpas that served as the mayor of their small town fifty years ago, parents who are lifelong friends with the Clintons (true story), or relatives who were the founders of the local party. That's not me. Not by a longshot. I am not someone who has spent even a large fraction of my life engaged in party politics and activism. I basically walked in off the street with a bunch of great ideas and moxie and threw my hat in the ring. I thought the only folks I had to win over were other normies, like myself. You know, the voters.

Well, the fact of the matter is that party politics and local activism is sort of powered by the Gatekeepers. Now, I don't mean this in a pejorative sense at all. These people are incredible stalwarts of democracy and electoral or social engagement. The Gatekeepers, I discovered, are unsung heroes who volunteer their time to run major clubs and organizations around the city and have put in the blood, sweat, and tears to make sure the Democratic Party has the local presence and power to make things happen at every level of government.

They're also a tough crowd to please, and you better show up with your A-game when trying to woo them and win their support. I'll never forget meeting Rufi, a true powerhouse and force to be reckoned with here in our local Democratic Party's office. Upon first meeting me she asked, "So what is it that you have to offer to this race and why should I consider voting for you? You know, Todd's got a lot going for him, so what makes you a good candidate, too?"

Damn, girl. Imma need some aloe for that sick, sick, burn! I had literally declared my candidacy only a couple weeks prior, and Rufi was my first taste of what it meant to be an actual candidate on the trail. I like to think I handled myself well in that moment, answering in great detail why I believed I brought a fresh voice to the race as a young woman of color, and walked away having earned at least a little bit of her respect. I mean, now we're practically BFFs (right, Rufi?!), so I'd say I did.

▶ **Moral of the story:** These people's acceptance and approval isn't everything, but you'll need to get to know them and work with them to make headway as a candidate and become a future political leader of any sort.

Your Family and Friends

Running for office and doing this crazy big, unpredictable, exhausting thing really shows you not only who you are but also who your Family and Friends are. You're going to meet completely new versions of people you've known for years and years, and it's not always going to be great. But, unless they're extra shitty, I hope you can find a way to forgive them if they suck. And if they surprise you by supporting you in ways you couldn't have anticipated, I hope you'll remember to let them know how lucky you are that they're in your life, especially during such an incredible moment in time.

▶ **Moral of the story:** Don't forget the people who helped you get where you are.

I 've always prided myself on being a pretty good judge of character. I can spend a couple minutes talking with someone and have them all figured out like *that* *snaps fingers, smugly*.

During my nannying years as a college student, I remember feeling a tinge of "idk she seems hella cray" about one of the moms I'd come across during after-school pick-ups and play-dates. She was friendly enough, but her chattiness was always peppered with comments about being rich but unhappy or marrying up, and I'd be left standing there, staring so hard at the children I was being paid to watch that my contacts would start drying out because I wasn't blinking, praying for the earth to open up and swallow me whole to save me from the awkward and inappropriate conversation being forced upon me. At twenty-two years old, I was ill-equipped to handle the inevitably weird conversations that come from being around obscenely wealthy people. Turns out, she was a literal burglar and had been robbing the multimillion-dollar houses of her neighbors and friends.

See. I can smell cray-cray a mile away.

Every so often, though, someone will surprise me. Even the folks I've known for years.

Like any other campaign, we had volunteers, interns, and staff. But the members of my campaign who surprised me the most were the people in my immediate orbit who I never asked for help but were there for me even before I knew I needed them. For months, this group of people showed up all over Houston, wearing their Silky for Congress t-shirts not only to every campaign and political event around town but also in their regular lives.

My campaign staff and volunteers became so recognizable that the campaign manager of one of my opponents half-snarked to Imran that we were so hard to get rid of, we were a *squad*—The Silky Squad.

Obviously, that nickname is so baller, shot caller we put it on t-shirts *immediately*.

★

"Hey champ! How's it going?"

Every day, for the more than one hundred days of my campaign, this is the first thing I'd hear on the other end of the line. Hell or high water, Lee made sure to call me or come by my house to check-in. Whether he intended to or not, his unwavering dedication and belief in me made him one of the founding members of The #SilkySquad.

If every obnoxious 1980s movie character played by Dan Ackroyd, John Candy, Chevy Chase, and Jim Belushi had a baby, and you gave that baby a law degree, an eidetic memory, an incredibly high IQ, and a heart of gold, this gruff, sweet, smart, hilarious, baby-man would be Lee. An Army vet with an imposing stature (and the palest white guy I have ever seen) and a slight drawl when he speaks, you half expect Lee to say a whole lot of dumb, Fox News bullshit when you first meet him.[13] While he does say a lot of ridiculous shit, he's as lefty of a liberal as they come. Policy advisor and part-time body man, Lee used his lawyering skills while accompanying me on the trail to put racists, misogynists, fascists, and all-around-fuck-wits in their place. It wasn't uncommon for people to remark to Lee about "that Indian girl running for Congress" and "what if she's a Muslim," only for him to shut that nonsense down with a quickness. I may have initially thought he was a serial killer, but it turned out he was a yellow dog Democrat who used his white male privilege for good.

Over the span of four months, I would come to learn a lot about Lee. Descending from a long line of Ohioan politicos, Lee's belief in and desire for a government that works for all of us paralleled my own in ways we couldn't have predicted when we met at Axelrad that day. He's also loyal to a fault, and despite trying to pretend he's a grumpy misanthrope, he's as much of a believer in the basic goodness of people as I am. Once he's decided y'all are friends, he's got your back for life. I had no idea when he offered to help me as a policy advisor that I was also getting a political ringer—his eidetic memory combined with both a granular and macro understanding of American politics allowed me to fill in my own knowledge gaps. I'm not a lawyer, and I wasn't a poli sci major, so I had to learn a lot on the fly about the nitty-gritty of politics. Lee was my walking, talking encyclopedia on anything I needed help understanding. And the best thing about Lee is that he is

---

13 I blame his shaved head, and a year-round wardrobe comprised of khaki cargo shorts, hiking boots, and camo hat for making him look like a Trump-loving Republican.

a teacher at heart. Never one to give a single sentence reply to an important question, he'd go in-depth on nearly everything I wasn't fully clear or informed on. My four months on the trail with him at my side was a crash-course in applied political science.

Lee also has this knack for swooping in and offering an assist at the exact right moment. In the first week of my campaign, I was asked to take a lunch with someone who wanted to see how they could use their technological know-how to help my campaign. Being a *candidate* felt weird and borderline fraudulent, and I had a hard time leaning into this new role. I thought I'd have a few weeks of being a candidate in private before having to go out and be one in front of, like, actual people! I still hadn't automated my stump speech and candidate spiel, and so during that lunch when the gentleman asked, "Why'd you decide to jump into the race?" I suddenly got flustered and couldn't articulate my words. Lee saw I was floundering and saved me from looking like an idiot, without making it obvious that I was having some sort of an aneurysm. Anytime I'd freak out a tiny bit at what it meant to run for office, Lee would talk me off the edge of self-doubt and hype me up like he was being paid to do so. He wasn't. Homeboy *volunteered full-time* on my campaign as policy advisor.

Lee treats me like the kid sister he loves palling around with but is too cool to say so.

Here in Texas, we get to vote early for about two weeks prior to Election Day. Ideally, a candidate would have representation at every polling location in the geographical area they're running to represent. In Harris County, there are about fifty-two early voting locations; on Election Day that number jumps to roughly 757 polling centers. Yeah, Texas is hella big, y'all.

Realistically speaking, it's nearly impossible for any campaign to staff each of the fifty-two early voting locations with a volunteer from 7:00 a.m. to 7:00 p.m. seven days a week for two weeks. Instead, what most campaigns do is make sure there's a volunteer at each of the ten busiest locations during the early voting period. It's a lot to ask of people to give up part (or even all) of their day to stand in the Texas heat and pass out campaign push cards and fliers to voters for hours on end. While there are many inspiring people that are worth handing out push cards for—even if it means getting the middle finger from Republican voters and a nasty farmer's tan from the Texas sun—I definitely did not think I was one of those people.

Like I said earlier, when you're running for office, there are going to be so many people who will hardcore believe in you and schlep for you that you never expected. Much to my complete and utter surprise, my sister-in-law, Sana, was one of those very people.

Having moved to Houston from Pakistan only a year and a half prior to my campaign launch in October 2017, Sana and I had never really gotten to spend a whole lot of time together. Even though I've known my in-laws since high school, Sana had always lived overseas, which meant we didn't know each other very well. I loved her because she was my family, but we weren't BFFs or anything.

Before I really got to know her, I saw Sana as this tiny, slim, demure woman who measured her words before she spoke, was polished and fancier than I could ever be, and carried herself with poise and grace. Her life back in Pakistan was basically physician by day and fancypants socialite by night. It didn't even occur to me to ask if she'd be a part of my campaign since I assumed she was too cool to even want to. Turns out, I didn't even have to ask.

The night of my campaign launch, she showed up with two dozen blue and white balloons and then stayed after to help us clean and pack up. This normally reserved woman turned up the charm and mingled with total randos the whole night just to hype me up and make me look good. For the next four months, Sana showed up to ninety-five percent of my campaign events. Sometimes these events were a total dud and no one really showed up, but in my case, I always at least had Sana there to be my wing woman.

During the two weeks of early voting, Sana showed up nearly every day to volunteer at the polls for me without me even asking her to. I'm talking about ten-hour days in ninety-degree Texas heat. When she first asked if I needed some help, I assumed she'd come down for an hour or two one weekday when it was convenient for her. Nope. Instead, she practically put her entire life on hold for fourteen days and drove into town from Sugar Land (a suburb of Houston nearly an hour away) to hand out push cards and engage with voters on my behalf.

I had always seen our relationship as that of normal, run-of-the-mill sisters-in-law. But, as cheesy as it sounds, after what she did for me and my campaign, I knew I had an actual *sister* in her. Even to this day, I am confounded over what I could have possibly done to deserve such unfaltering love and support from a person I hardly even knew. In those few months of my campaign, I saw in Sana the kind of family member I wanted to be, and I am forever grateful for her encouragement and help at a time when I needed it most but was too shy to ask.

I have known my brother-in-law, Omer, since we were in high school. Two grades above me, he and his crew would walk the halls six bros wide, simultaneously looking hella cool and being inconsiderate of the rest of us trying to rush to class before the tardy bell rang.

Dressed exclusively in fancy mall brands like Armani Exchange *and* Emporio Armani, his neck-length hair slicked back, a pen tucked behind his ear, and carrying a single, folded-up spiral notebook with nary a backpack in sight, I often wondered how he continuously avoided detention or sparkle duty[14] despite being such a freaking rule breaker. During English class one day, I saw Omer walk past our classroom

---

14 For those good kids who never got in trouble, sparkle duty is when you're forced into slave labor during lunch period and you have to go from table to table collecting other students' garbage. Your sparkle duty isn't considered finished until you've collected two garbage bags full of trash.

door and nudged Imran (who I had a crush on at the time) to "look at that scary-ass looking dude wandering the halls like a truant. Shouldn't he be in class!?"

Turns out Omer was Imran's brother. Omer also turned out to be the Felix Unger to my Oscar Madison.[15] Ever since we were teens, Omer's one job in life has been to tease me relentlessly for being an uptight nerd and the patron saint of lost causes—an accurate descriptor and a badge of honor I wear proudly—while I mock him for having the personality of an Instagram influencer account and the moral compass of Jeff Bezos.

For instance, at the time of writing this, Omer's life's aspirations include becoming a Tik-Tok celebrity and figuring out a way to exit his future wedding in a helicopter, not off of a helipad like a normal person, but from in front of the wedding venue so that all the wedding guests can actually *see* how much of a baller he is.

On the night of my campaign kickoff party, Omer showed up with Najam, the owner of Pakistan Times USA, a paper with a weekly circulation of about 40,000 American households. Photographer in tow, Najam stayed the entire evening and documented the whole event! Apparently, Najam loved my "spunkiness" so much he ran a half-page spread in his paper about me and my campaign a couple weeks later.

---

15 For my younger millennial and gen z readers, this is a reference to an old-timey TV show and movie called The Odd Couple. Check it out (but avoid the mid-2000s reboot with Chandler from Friends because that was terrible). It's hilarious!

I may have been a non-Muslim Indian woman running in a congressional district with an Asian population of less than four percent, and publicity in a Pakistani newspaper probably wasn't going to help me get any votes for the primary, but I'll be damned if I didn't feel like literally the most famous person in the world after seeing myself in a newspaper!

Not even two weeks later, I get a call from Omer. "Get ready, you have a TV interview in two hours at the Pakistani news station." Omer and I do not share the same politics at all (in fact, we argue frequently about politics at our weekly Sunday night dinners), and yet, without me even asking (or thinking to ask) he reached out to his network, called in some favors, and got me my first television interview.

Imagine my surprise the day he randomly showed up to my house asking for stacks of push cards to put on cars all around my district. For several weeks he did this, covering the 300-plus square miles of my district several times over. Voters would attend my candidate meet and greets from all over Houston after hearing about my campaign from a card left on their car at H-E-B or church.

As a total nobody running for Congress, finding enough volunteers to do literature drops eight hours a day all around the district and securing free press and media coverage is not easy. And honestly, I had no idea how to even go about it those first few weeks of my campaign.

Omer stepping up on his own to support me and my candidacy legitimized my campaign in a way that caused others to take notice of what I was doing. He may have thought I was a bleeding-heart liberal determined to fix the world, destined to discover it was un-fixable, but Omer believed in me and what I stood for. When I tried to get all sentimental and thank him for everything he was doing to help me, he just sort of gave me a nod and said, "Nah, don't worry about it." Him working in the background expecting zero thanks or recognition is precisely why he's the *only* person who gets to request one special main dish *and* dessert at my Thanksgiving dinner for the rest of our lives.

I first met Courtney in 2015 through Brenda and her husband Jay.[16] Courtney was one of those people who was *so* incredibly sweet and nice that I *totally* thought she was full of shit and faking it or something because how can someone be *that* nice *and* positive all the time? You know those people who tend to be energy vampires? Someone who leaves you feeling exhausted or even sorta blah and negative when you hang out with them, but you can't pinpoint why? Courtney is the total opposite of that: she's got this "Bob Ross meets Mr. Rogers" energy that makes her a joy to be around.

She talks about people and places in a way that's positive and very glass half-full. She doesn't snark on folks, even when they TOTALLY deserve it. She speaks with zero pretense and doesn't judge people, even when they TOTALLY deserve it.

---

16 "Jay" is short for Jabroni because that's what he is. A fucking Jabroni.

Her patience could rival that of a monk, something I witnessed first hand when she explained to Brenda, in multiple ways, why affirmative action wasn't racist to white men (I, however, was whatever the opposite of a patient monk is during this idiotic conversation).

At first, I tried hard to keep myself from liking or becoming friends with her. I like to rant and rage at all the things I find unjust or immoral, and I, wrongly, assumed Courtney, with all that sunshine and cheer shining out of her ass, would be full of useless, toxic positivity. Remember, I fancy myself too emo and too edgy to be hanging out with happy-go-lucky people when I want to be cranky and rage-y about the world.

When Brenda suggested that Courtney start meeting us for our twice-a-week workout at Memorial Park (walking is a workout, right?), I was kind of hesitant but decided to be cool with it as opposed to being a dick and refusing to share my BFF walking time with another person.

The three of us spent the bulk of 2015 and 2016 going for walks two to three times a week, all the while shooting the shit about our lives. After the 2016 election, nearly three-quarters of our three-and-a-half mile walk would consist of me ranting about Trump and whatever headline was dominating that day's news cycle: the Newsweek Interview, Russia, secret meetings at the Trump Tower (with Russia), Stormy Daniels, and more collusion with Russia. At first, Courtney and Brenda pretty much listened to me rant, but over the course of our walking dates, Courtney chimed in more and more and I realized just how much our values and beliefs were aligned.

A few years younger than me, Courtney had a wealth of knowledge about tons of social issues, helping me to become even more "woke" than I was before. Like when she took me to task for not fully understanding the issue of "Pink Pussy hats" and trans erasure. Our evening walks began to take on a new purpose as we pushed and challenged one another on how we saw the world and our place in fixing the problems we talked about week after week.

When I decided to run for office, I never expected that Courtney would literally become both my field director *and* campaign manager after my first campaign manager quit unexpectedly. Courtney was doing a million things at once for the campaign, from setting up tables at campaign events to block walking with me when we didn't have enough volunteers to go out on certain weekends. She even made phone calls to recruit volunteers and book event venues during her lunch break at work. Courtney showed up to everything and constantly blew me away with how dedicated and excited she was to be part of my team.

I don't know what we would have done without her. Of all the friendships and relationships I've ever had, Courtney will forever hold a special place in my heart, right next to Spanx, Rent The Runway, and Taco Bell. For a short time, on an unexpectedly wild adventure, she was my total ride or die.

Layla and I met in Kuala Lumpur, Malaysia in late 2014 while volunteering for a large women's charitable organization: the Association of British Women, Malaysia.

I'd heard through another member that Layla was from Texas, so I essentially stalked her by joining the events planning committee because I was incredibly homesick and decided I wanted to be friends with another Texan. After meeting for lunch to talk about joining her committee, she mentioned being from Houston, and unbeknownst to her, she was now my Malaysia BFF. Later, we both discovered we hated living in Malaysia (it's so hot and sticky, and the food isn't great, and did I mention HOW HOT IT IS?!), which is pretty uncommon when meeting other expatriates. You're basically a pariah if you're the one expat who isn't constantly fangirling the country you're living in, forcing you to suffer silently because you don't have anyone to snark on things with.

After palling around Kuala Lumpur for the better part of a year, we both found ourselves moving back to Houston within six months of each other. Almost two years later, I filed to run for office and wouldn't you know it, Layla's new home was in my congressional district!

Now, her having two kids at home, both under three years old, meant I wasn't going to ask her for much help with my campaign. Although we had been friends for about three years, I didn't think we were total BFFs (outside of Malaysia, obvs) or anything, and I certainly didn't feel like I could just pile stuff onto her already super-busy life by asking for help with my campaign. When Layla and her husband James asked how they could help, I tasked them with something I thought was easy and manageable: hosting a small meet and greet for me with their friends in the district.

To my surprise, Layla asked me for a list of houses in her area she could block walk. All casual and chill, she said it would be easy for her to walk her neighborhood with the kids in their stroller, and plus, "the weather was good nowadays, and it would be a nice way to get some exercise in."

Like a one-woman army, toddlers in tow, with hundreds of houses to hit up, Layla took several packets from me and block walked her area day after day amongst the busyness of her regular life. She initiated conversations with her friends and neighbors about politics—a definite first for her and a no-no for liberals here in Houston, where it's easy to leave a bad taste in your neighbor's or co-worker's mouth by outing yourself as a Democrat. Before I knew it, thanks to Layla, I had gotten a nice little stronghold in this precinct, with my signs all over the area.

Prior to my run, Layla and I had never talked politics, so her schlepping all over her little corner of Houston for me took me by surprise and made me see her for the lowkey, loyal homie that she was. After that, I forced her to be my stateside BFF not only because she was from Texas, but also because she's a total badass. Stateside BFF duties include, but are not limited to: participating in a rug exchange program wherein we trade rugs with one another whenever we get tired of our own; being brutally honest about the fact that I need to be more responsible about how much stuff I'm buying from Lululemon;

shaming one another's husbands for hoarding ugly furniture; being a riveted audience member for her girls' living room ballet performances; and dropping off homemade baked goods at her house because I can't be trusted NOT to eat an entire pound cake in two days.

Making friends in one's thirties isn't easy. The shared adventures and experiences that are effortless in the friendships from high school and college just aren't there when you're older and married and a parent.[17] So I'm pretty stoked I somehow beat the odds and found another bestie even though I'm an oldie!

For most of high school, Wes and I were best friends. This was *way* before cell phones, so we would often communicate between classes by putting long notes in each other's lockers to read and later reply to during class. Active in many clubs and working hard to make good grades, we fancied ourselves way too cool for school, rocking our ball chain necklaces, wearing men's white undershirts like they were *actual shirts*, and getting dressed up for the homecoming football game but not actually going to the dance itself. We were very ironic, y'all.

---

17 Hey there young reader! I promise adulthood isn't bad like I'm making it sound here! I love being a grown-up, but I'd be lying if I said I didn't miss being able to see and hang out with my friends more than once a quarter. But hey, when you're old, you always get a good turnout for your birthday because your friends now have kids, and they'll be desperate to finally get a night out on the town, and your birthday party will probably be the one night that year they'll splurge on a sitter.

Rebels without a cause that we were, the alternative stylings of Linkin Park, Green Day, Blink-182, Fuel, Bush, The Strokes, and Tool became the soundtrack of our freshman and sophomore year best-friendship. Both of us had strict parents who didn't want us mingling too much with friends of the opposite sex, so we'd often make up elaborate lies in order to sneak out to concerts with our group of friends. If there were classes to be skipped and hallways to be aimlessly roamed, you definitely wouldn't have called us because we would not have joined in such truancy!

Because social media wasn't a thing when we graduated in 2002, Wes and I had a hard time staying in touch after high school. We would run into each other once in a while around Sugar Land during our college years, but never really saw one another again. Until Facebook. Around 2014, I saw that Wes was a teacher in Mexico living his best life. I was a little jealous that he looked exactly the same as when we were kids (not ONE wrinkle or grey hair? What the hell, Wes?!), but he was fluent in Spanish now and was this fun teacher with all these great friends, hanging out on the beach with hot dudes holding fancy drinks with umbrellas in them. You don't always know how folks you once knew ended up, so seeing an old friend doing well brought me a lot of happiness.

In March of 2018, during early voting for the primary, I put out a call for volunteers to be stationed at the various voting locations around town. I was more than a little shocked when Wes messaged me asking if he could volunteer and do a few shifts at a polling location. I honestly couldn't believe it. Mainly because I THOUGHT HE STILL LIVED IN MEXICO! I hadn't talked to him in more than a decade and to see that message from him nearly moved me to tears. Because his schedule was so busy, he wasn't going to be able to swing by and pick up his *Silky for Congress* t-shirt, push cards, etc. So he suggested we drop everything off in a bag on his mom's porch, five minutes from our old high school stomping grounds. It was so late at night when we were finally able to get out to Sugar Land and drop it off that I couldn't even text to see if Wes was awake to say "Hi" after all these years. The next day he posted pictures of himself on Facebook in the Silky Squad shirt, holding push cards, standing outside of Houston Community College's polling station.

Kenny and I had neighboring lockers during our junior and senior years of high school. I never really talked to him because he totally gave off an "Asian Ferris Bueller" vibe, what with the cool sports car and all the girls who liked him always nonchalantly idling around waiting for him, thereby blocking me from getting to my own damn locker. We didn't become friends until our senior year when our individual friend groups overlapped. Back in the olden days, there were no cellphones and thus no texting or FaceTiming, so Kenny and I would spend hours talking on the phone about movies and books. He was that friend who would say, "Oh my God, you haven't seen High Fidelity yet? I have the video at home; you'll have to come over after school today and watch it!" To this day, anytime I see Matthew Broderick or John Cusack on TV, I'm reminded to shoot a text to Kenny and his wife Cynthia saying, "Hey, how's it going? Miss y'all!"

Out of our group of friends, Kenny was always the least likely to talk politics and religion. After high school and all through college and grad school, he and I would always find time to meet for lunch and chat about everything in our lives: his newest girlfriend, Imran's latest job, his LSAT studying, my latest "should I apply to grad school" conundrum. And yet, if you'd asked me back then what his political leanings were, I wouldn't have had the foggiest idea because he never really brought it up, and back then I didn't care enough about politics to ask.

For the entirety of my campaign, event after event, Kenny and Cynthia showed up to every single one. They brought friends with them, hyped me up to total strangers, and basically made me feel so extra loved that I couldn't *not* believe in myself. Sometimes it can feel weird to put yourself out there in front of people who have known you half your life: they've seen you at your worst, your silliest, your chubbiest (me at twenty-one years old), and your most awkward. These two, whom I adored and respected so much, believed in me and came out week after week to be part of the Silky Squad. I never told them how much their support meant to me, but it meant everything.

It baffles me at times just how little we know people. Considering none of the Silky Squad had ever been outspoken about politics, or even really politically active outside of voting, I never expected them to care enough to get involved in my campaign, especially since I was too self-conscious to ask those closest to me for help.

Ironically, while they all believed in me, I guess I didn't return the favor. I assumed these people—who love me so much—didn't care about me enough to help me when I needed it the most. I regret not putting the same faith in them that they had in me.

The unpredictable human factor has been my favorite part of the mostly shitty world of politics. People continue to surprise me. Sometimes it can be easy to feel cynical about the messiness of this country's government and the disingenuousness of our elected officials, but, especially after my own campaign, I've got an unlimited supply of faith and hope in people. My time on the trail reaffirmed my belief that we aren't too far gone as a country.

Don't get me wrong. The last four years have been a clusterfuck/dumpster fire/shitshow rolled into one, but when people who never thought twice about their role in government and politics can be moved to get involved, even without being asked, then there's still hope we can turn this clusterfuck/dumpster fire/shitshow around.

*Best Friends (not) Forever

"**S**ilky! There is a *literal* WAR on white men!"

It was after midnight and Brenda's birthday party had just come to a screeching halt. Standing in her dining room, her husband Jay[18] drunkenly yelling at me and Imran about how *hard* it was to be a white person in the year 2018, I knew deep down in my heart that our friendship was all but dead.

Brenda and I met in an Introduction to Poetry class at the University of Houston. Looking for an elective that seemed interesting but not too involved and labor-intensive, I'd signed up for the class over a week late. That first day, Brenda mouthed to me from across the table that my haircut was cool. We both basically had the same style: the "Posh Spice" bob that was VERY in vogue in 2006. Years later, I learned from Brenda that her secret to breaking the ice to make new friends is to give them a compliment. That was just one of the many things she would teach me over the next fourteen years or so.

After class, we exchanged phone numbers so that I could Xerox some pages out of her poetry textbook while I waited for mine to be delivered. A couple days later, we texted and I agreed to meet her in front of the library at three o'clock. Young Silky was a total flake and completely forgot to meet her, leaving the poor girl out there waiting for me for half an hour before giving up and going home. I didn't even call or text her!

---

18 Friendly reminder that Jay is short for Jabroni because that's what he is. A fucking Jabroni.

Jesus. I was such a rude shit. But because Brenda is wired to see the best in people, she never even mentioned me blowing her off that day. The following week, I awkwardly tried to avoid eye contact with her in class because I felt awful for being a flake, but she acted like nothing ever happened, and that small act of kindness kicked off one of the most important and significant relationships of my adult life.

Fourteen years later, over Gchat, I was practically begging her to be my campaign manager. It was ONLY going to be a temporary gig, I assured her, only until I hired someone. And, come on, how could I possibly do this without her? I can't run for Congress without my best friend!

Since our early twenties, we had been through everything together: engagements; weddings; co-hosting baby showers; first post-college jobs and subsequent work drama, then the inevitable existential career crisis that would follow; two international moves (me); a divorce (her); a miscarriage (me); car wrecks; bad hair cuts (bangs—both of us); post-grad work; buying and selling houses; gaining and losing twenty pounds each (several times); and one Warrior Dash obstacle race where we literally ran through mud and fire, side-by-side.

There are moments when I wonder whether the untimely demise of our best friendship was my fault. I never should have asked Brenda to be part of my campaign. After all, for as long as I had known her, she had absolutely loathed talking or even thinking about politics. So, out of respect for her, I always made sure not to talk politics with or around her. And honestly, it really wasn't hard to do. With so much to talk about, politics was easy to ignore, especially in the world prior to the 2016 election cycle. After that fateful election night in November 2016, however, the intersection between social justice issues and politics consumed my every waking moment.

The problem I now faced was that, as a native Texan who still lived in Texas, I was constantly surrounded by decent, salt-of-the-earth folks who "don't see color and just wish we could all get along." For the first time in my life, being around moderates and conservatives felt akin to being in an episode of the *Twilight Zone*. Overnight, I became someone else. I've always been a "bleeding-heart hippie liberal" like my Republican dad used to call me. But now I couldn't keep my politics to myself. Whatever minuscule amount of chill I may have ever possessed was completely and entirely gone. I no longer gave the right-leaning moderates around me the benefit of the doubt that their shitty beliefs were because of naivete or a lack of information. Nope. If you believed "All Lives Matter" but that Black Lives don't, we had beef. Whatever already near-nonexistent filter I possessed had completely disappeared, and I had almost no control over the thoughts exiting my mouth. I decided it was my moral obligation to be a full-time Social Justice Warrior, extra emphasis on the Warrior bit. For all of 2016 and most of 2017, Daenerys Targaryen and her dragons had nothing on me.

Like millions of people across the United States, I got to work figuring out how I could #resist the Trump Administration. I got on the email lists of the newly formed online organization Indivisible and the activist app Daily Action, both of which were created to help Americans fight Trump's assault on the Constitution. I attended every march and protest and did anything I could think of to be a constant voice of dissent during what I knew was a historical moment in time, full of serious threat and distress.

Here and there, I tried talking with Brenda about current events and the never-ending onslaught of political bombs making the daily news. I would always strive to explain the facts of what was going on and what it meant for Americans. I remember having dinner at Zoe's Kitchen after going walking at our favorite spot, Memorial Park, and Brenda asking, "Ok, so, I don't get why it's *bad* for the President to talk or communicate with Russia? Isn't he *supposed* to talk to the leaders of other countries?" This was early 2017 and info on the Trump Tower meeting had just made headlines around the world.

Still, not all felt lost. Friends don't have to agree on everything to be friends, right?

2017 sort of passed in a blur. I spent the first half of the year traveling around the country for various political trainings and a couple of Democratic conventions. I was all in, constantly meeting new people, joining new activist groups, completely immersed in Democratic politics nearly every night of the week.

By October of 2017, I had fully decided to run for office. I then broke our unspoken "no politics" rule and asked Brenda to be my campaign manager. She said no to me several times until I finally did a very un-Silky-like thing and literally begged her to be by my side as I did the scariest thing I've ever done. I was completely sincere and dead serious when I told her that I absolutely couldn't do this without my best friend.

What a lot of folks might not realize about running for office (at least I didn't until I ran) is how little you discuss politics when you're a candidate. Don't get me wrong, you talk about policy and your ideas for making things better, but those charged, emotional, and heated discussions just aren't the norm when you're on the trail. This is probably why Brenda stuck around as my campaign manager as long as she did.

Heck, by the time March rolled around, she'd become slightly interested in the political process herself, proudly donning a *Beto for Texas* t-shirt at the start of 2018. What I didn't see coming, though, was the slow, almost painless death of our friendship, symbolically represented by a Ted Cruz sign prominently displayed in her front yard later that same year during the November midterms.

In a little over six months, my best friend of nearly fourteen years went from a moderate Democrat—she voted for Hillary, Lizzie Fletcher (a Democrat running for Congress who unseated an entrenched Republican from a seat that hadn't been held by a Dem for almost fifty years), and Beto in the March primary—to a Ted Cruz supporter.

At her birthday party in November 2018, right before the primary election, she half jokingly pleaded with her birthday party attendees to "please don't stop being friends with us" after her husband Jay stopped the party dead in its tracks by loudly proclaiming "there is a literal war on white men in this country." We ended up not seeing each other for several months after that night. But we still chatted online and texted like things were normal, as though her husband hadn't recently outed himself as a sympathizer to the alt-right.

By the summer of 2019, with my failed primary bid more than a year behind me, our friendship was all but dead. The final death knell rang when her husband began brigading the comments section of my Facebook posts on Planned Parenthood and reproductive rights.

I've been a reproductive and abortion rights advocate since I learned about Roe v. Wade when I was thirteen years old. After I lost the primary in March of 2018, I reached out to my new political and activist friends and got more involved with Planned Parenthood. What still baffles me is that at the beginning of 2019, I sent a Planned Parenthood job description to Brenda to look over because I thought that Director of Education could be a great fit for me. Over Gchat, she enthusiastically agreed, telling me I was perfect for the role.

I had always known Brenda was anti-choice, often chalking it up to her Catholic upbringing. Her husband, when I met him, was apolitical and almost an atheist. He hadn't even voted in the 2016 election! Yet, somehow, not even two years later, his edge-lord jabroni ass was supporting Tea Party Ted Cruz and yelling on Facebook—first on his wall, where NOBODY would reply, and then on the comment section of *my* posts, hoping to get a reaction—that life began at conception, advocating for the jailing of women and doctors involved in the abortion process.

During and after the campaign, Brenda and I rarely talked politics, but it seemed that my political activism had awakened something not-so-great in Jay. He suddenly couldn't stop himself from trying to engage me in political discourse. Overcome with anger at a Black football player kneeling during the national anthem, he began texting me and chatting with me on Gchat nonstop. He would randomly send me links to articles, then practically demand that I reply with my opinion on whatever he had just sent me. When I would reply, he would vehemently disagree and then further demand that I defend my stance by presenting him with a rebuttal filled with FActS AnD LOg!C!! It wasn't long before I started to ignore his attempts at these types of conversations. I went so far as to tell him that since I had lost my race, I was under no obligation to talk with him about politics or policy. His tax dollars weren't paying my salary; I was a civilian just like him, and not a public servant. So back the fuck off, dude.

But he didn't. Instead, my refusal to engage caused him to become incensed, and he doubled down. Anytime I would visit Brenda and her new baby, Jay would try and goad me into talking politics by randomly blurting out Fox News headlines in my general direction NONSTOP.

Soon after Brenda had given birth, we all met at La Madeleine near her son's pediatrician's office for brunch:

Me: *about to bite into my french toast*

Jabroni: *phone chimes with a news update* Oh, wow. The Honduran migrants are making their way toward our southern border. What do you think about that, Silky?

Me: *Cooing at their three-month-old baby, trying to get him to smile* Huh? Oh, wow, that is crayyyyy.

Rinse and repeat for the next eight months on every idiotic, hyper-partisan, mostly fabricated news topic Fox News had decided was important that day.

Over the last few months, I've thought so much about how our friendship ended the way it did, with Brenda posting a strange, attacking comment on a Facebook post announcing my upcoming work to help organize the annual Roe v. Wade Luncheon here in Houston. Considering Brenda was never the type of person to be uncouth or inappropriate in public, her essentially calling some of our mutual friends "baby murderers" made the entire exchange that much more freaking bizarre. For the next few days, nearly half of our sixty mutual friends sent me texts completely aghast over Brenda's suddenly weird and out-of-character behavior. In all the years we'd known each other, I had never seen her act like such a fool.

Always the epitome of southern propriety and politeness, Brenda taught me the importance of having a verbal filter and how it isn't always necessary to say what's on my mind, especially if it's hurtful. Much of the person I've become is because of my friendship with her. She spent years being my role model for how to handle and navigate life's awkward social interactions with the utmost southern grace and charm. I once told her that I often thought "what would Brenda do" when

I found myself stumped about how to deal with certain social and familial situations because she always knew just the right thing to say.

Over and over, Brenda showed me the power of killing folks with kindness and how important giving people the benefit of the doubt was. She had an interesting ability to help me see the world in a less negative way. Through her example, I learned how to be a good family member to my own family and in-laws. She had not one ounce of jealousy in her whole body; there was none of that frenemies nonsense that can be so common between young women. Instead, she was my full-time cheerleader. While she always had my back and took my side, she was also my in-house counsel—the perpetual devil's advocate—forcing me to be honest with myself even when I didn't want to be. I always told her that the only person who knew me better than her was Imran, who I met in high school. My years of friendship with her made me a better person. No one was more blindsided by the end of our friendship than I was.

It's taken me a while to realize that the story of our breakup is intertwined with the story of my run for Congress. A huge part of me feels like the *only* bad thing that came out of running for office was how it somehow killed one of the most important relationships in my life. I often wonder if I had not run, would we still be best friends, and would I still be Aunt Silky to her sons? Before I threw my hat into the ring, my biggest fear was stepping into the ridiculous world of politics and losing myself. Never in a million years did I think that I'd instead lose my best friend.

THAT TIME I ATE A

COLD, DAY OLD TACO BELL *Burrito*

Lee: Oh. My. God. What are you *doing*?!

Me, at my kitchen counter, well past midnight: What?

Visibly grossed out and very dramatic Lee: Dude. That's really gross. Aren't you at least going to heat it up?! God. Ew. How old is it?

Me, mouth full: Huh? Nah. It's fine. I'm starving, man. I have not eaten, like, anything all day. Plus it's only from yesterday, and I am not gonna let a good burrito go to waste!

And to be honest, it wasn't half bad.

Why is it that we as a society are okay with people eating cold pizza out of the fridge, or even cold fried chicken, but heaven forbid someone eats a cold Taco Bell bean burrito ONCE, and it becomes your former policy advisor's go-to party anecdote for all eternity?!

At least twice on the trail, I had to sneak off to the bathroom and wash queso out of my hair. Leaning forward trying to grab some chips from the basket, I instead dunked my hair in the personal bowl of queso in front of me. I basically had to stop eating in public for the rest of the campaign after the second cheesy hair incident.

Speaking of hair, one time I went to get my hair washed and blown-out for a candidate debate, and within five minutes of sitting down, I fell asleep for the entire appointment. I nearly fell out of my chair twice during my forty-five-minute nap and woke up with drool all over the side of my face. Although I didn't ask, the stylist kindly reassured me that because I wasn't snoring too loudly she was almost totally sure no one else in the salon heard me.

Being on the campaign trail is exhausting and super not glamorous. Thanks to hair blowouts and Spanx, I was able to look like I had my shit together, but it was all mostly an illusion. Running for office is all about faking it 'til you make it (or faking it 'til you don't make it and then writing about your burrito and queso escapades in a book)!

"YOU
LIKE ME,
YOU REALLY
like ME!"

(LOL JK, JK,
Everyone
Hates Me)

"*T*hat's weird—why isn't my sign in their yard anymore? I could have sworn I saw it there yesterday.*"

Later that evening, while out block walking in my neighborhood with my husband, he knocked on their door to ask them if they needed another sign. Not even two weeks prior, I'd canvassed that same house and had an awesome and lengthy conversation with the guy who lived there. He wasn't really into politics, mostly because he felt that Congress is overrun by career politicians who are only in it for themselves. The fact that I was a total newcomer to politics running on a progressive platform that I believed in had won him over, and he was super excited to put my sign in his yard. (Obviously, the missing yard sign was the work of some teenage rascals who perhaps channeled their budding interest in politics into petty theft and absconded with my sign in the dead of night only to proudly display it in their bedroom until they leave for college).

Imran: *Knock, knock* Hello! My name is Imran Malik, and I'm with the Silky Malik for Congress campaign. I was walking by while canvassing and noticed that your yard sign was missing and wanted to know if you'd like another one to replace it? Signs get stolen all the time, so I'm happy to bring you a new one. I have them in my car."

Friendly Neighborhood Voter: Oh, um, your sign wasn't stolen. We took it down and put it in the garage because we're supporting [opponent]. I didn't realize this, but apparently, my wife's mom is church friends with [opponent] and has even been volunteering on his campaign, so

I guess we're supporting him, too. I'm sorry. Your wife was really, really nice, and I'm rooting for her!

Imran: That's understandable. Thank you so much for holding on to the sign and not throwing it away! I can take it off your hands if you'd like. And hey, if you like Silky and you're rooting for her, I really hope you'll consider still voting for her in the primary!

Y'all, it sucks when you think you've earned someone's vote and then they take it back, even if they still like you or your platform. But ultimately, you can't take any of it too personally because it isn't personal. It's just politics.

Running for office can feel like a strange sort of popularity contest, one where there are no rules on how to win. Some people will vote for or support the candidate with the most charisma. Other people will vote for the candidate who has raised the most money, or who has the best platform. And then there are those who will vote for the candidate they think is the best looking/not too good looking/young enough/old enough, etc.

What was really jarring for me was the private support I kept getting from people who "couldn't" support me publicly unless I won the primary. It was like being the secret girlfriend who's too ugly to meet her boyfriend's friends. I mean, hey, thanks for thinking I'm great, and I'm really flattered you'll be voting for me in the primary, but it would also be helpful if you didn't keep that support a secret. So that, you know, *other* people might also support me.

However, despite the seemingly widespread, secret support I was earning from my fellow Houstonians (clearly not widespread enough to win the primary haha), the outpouring of real-life, public, tangible support that I *did* receive was overwhelming.

Like I mentioned earlier (I think I said it somewhere earlier; maybe I thought it and didn't type it out and now you, the reader, have no idea what I'm going on about. Man, is this book an emotional whirlwind or what?!), this whole running for office thing is a master class in the word "mercurial." Not only is "mercurial" one hell of a throwback to your SAT vocab flashcards, but it's also exactly what life is like on the campaign trail.

When you're running for office, you won't know how to feel about anything going on around you most of the time, primarily because everything around you—including the people you've known your whole life—is unpredictable. Unless you're Obama or a Kennedy, you really have no clue where you stand with voters much of the time.

You can waste so much mental energy continuously wondering whether the people you're talking to are rooting for you or rooting against you. And depending on which crowd you're in front of, you're probably right. If you're not careful, unimportant things like yard signs or endorsements can make running for office feel like a total mindfuck. And frankly, if you're going into politics because you want adoration and love (as opposed to wanting to make the world a better place), you're probably not the kind of person we need in office anyway.

SILKY FROM THE *Block*

The older I get, the more I truly understand JLo's "Jenny From the Block." Not only are we both raven-haired beauties often mistaken by racists for Mexican immigrants, but also like JLo, I am definitely living a much fancier life than I did as a kid or even a young adult. Until I was, like, twenty-five, I felt seriously awkward and uncomfortable walking into a Banana Republic because it was just a little *too* fancy for me. Nowadays, I've been known to buy stuff from Banana even when it's NOT on sale (not to brag). Like my own Indian American version of George and Weezy Jefferson, I'm moving on up, y'all!

Just the other day, I went to a fundraising dinner for a city council candidate, and when I walked in someone shouted, "Hey! I know you! You're famous!" Which, yes, was kind of cool, but also, if *I'm* famous, I feel like we need to redefine the word or something.

But also, I could legit BE famous and I would still feel like a political outsider and total nobody who ran for Congress, and I would wear that with a badge of honor. Maybe those of us with upbringings that are so different from life now have a hard time reconciling the two different experiences? I'm not sure. But, like Jenny From the Block, I still feel like Silky from the Block,[19] which is awesome and keeps me from ever taking myself or my sometimes-fancy surroundings too seriously. The only downside of this is that I often sell myself

---

19 Or, more accurately, Silky from the once-ratchet apartments on 5th Street, which are less ratchet now because Google Images is showing me the building has gotten a facelift and a pool! #MoCityRepresent

short and underestimate any influence I might have on the politics of my city.

I learned that maybe I wasn't a total nobody the first time I was asked for an endorsement. Not long after losing my primary election, I got an email from a wonderful woman, a candidate running for municipal office, asking if I would support her in her race. It was such an unexpected moment of affirmation, especially so soon after losing my election. I guess I wasn't some lame-o political failure after all, huh!

Except I was completely freaked out by the whole idea of *me* being someone whose endorsement would matter to anybody at all. I got way in my own head about it, too. Being a candidate seeking endorsements was a pretty comfortable space for me; the process sucked, sure, but it made sense that *I* was the one asking other, *important* people and organizations for their support. But the other way around? Felt a little fraudulent, to be honest.

So I did what any self-effacing woman does when confronted by their own insecurities: I made up some bullshit excuse about "not endorsing in a race with two or more Democratic female candidates" and noped right out of that whole situation.

What's sad to me is that even after doing this great big thing of running for office, I still didn't believe in myself. And because I couldn't recognize and appreciate all I had accomplished during my run, I couldn't understand why someone would want my endorsement, so I failed to support a woman who I believed in. Definitely not my proudest moment.

KEEP IT REAL,
KEEP IT CLASSY,
Y'all

W e were roughly a month away from the March primary, and I had just left Siphon Coffee near my house after finishing a meeting with an east coast politico, a friend of a friend, when I got the email.

> This investigation has led to a pending class-action lawsuit against [REDACTED] Loan Servicing, based on consumer reports about [REDACTED] business practices. Evidence suggests that there are a number of problems with the way [REDACTED] is collecting on certain loans. [REDACTED] is not properly crediting certain payments when made, it is force-placing insurance on certain loans, and it is charging fees and costs that are excessive and not proper according to state and federal law.

Unsure of whether the other candidates had seen or read it yet, I sent a group text asking them if they'd gotten the same email. Darrell, one of my Democratic primary opponents, had sent an email insinuating that the frontrunner's wealth was associated with some sort of shady money-lending-type family business.

Now, this might seem like an impotent attack, but I don't think "good" Democrats typically involve themselves with making money through predatory loan practices. I mean, obviously making money off being scummy is pretty non-partisan, but in a Democratic primary, it can be the kind of thing that knocks off enough votes to make a difference.

Darrell's email was, at least to me, sent to galvanize one of us into starting a smear campaign against Todd. It was similar to a "friend" who secretly hates you seeing your spouse at a restaurant with a person who is clearly a colleague, and then sending you a blurry pic of them laughing, with a follow-up text that reads, "If you ask me, having intimate afternoon 'lunches' with beautiful women is basically emotional infidelity, and I'd lawyer up fast, babe!!!!"

I suppose Darrell thought the rest of us would be foaming at the mouth for opposition research on Todd because he was the frontrunner. Instead, what he got was zero fanfare or intrigue and several 'reply all' emails saying, "Oh, wow. That's crazy town lol." I don't think he expected that none of us would take the bait.

After some quick and cursory Googling, it was obvious the whole thing was complete, fabricated nonsense. But still, even if the allegation *was* true, what was I supposed to do? Start a freaking smear campaign against my primary opponent? Don't get me wrong, airing dirty laundry has its place in politics. If we know terrible shit about someone running for office—sexual predators, tax evaders, pro-lifers who paid for their mistresses' abortions, the weekend cocaine fiend who enthusiastically supports the War on Drugs, homophobes with gay lovers— there's a moral obligation to put that hypocrite's business on blast. However, trying to make someone look bad by throwing random crap at the wall to see what sticks, all because it *might* help you win your primary, is pathetic and jacked up. But hey, if selling your soul just to win a congressional seat is worth it, then you do you, Voldemort. Just don't email me expecting I'll help peddle your toxicity.

I was super weirded out by the whole thing. I knew that I needed help; this was all way too low-level *House of Cards* for my taste, and I wasn't entirely sure of what to do. So still sitting in my car in the parking lot of Siphon, I called Lee and filled him in on my first brush with political drama. He confirmed what I felt in my gut: I needed to call the frontrunner and tell him what was going on so he could get ahead of this gossip before it could spread and reach voters.

While it might have been easier to ignore Darrell's email and walk away, not involving myself any further, something Lee said really underscored the importance of what was at stake in the 2018 midterm elections: "This kind of thing is bad for Democrats."

Lee was right. Hundreds of political newcomers across the country had stepped up to run for office not because they wanted prestige or glory, but, just like me, they wanted to change a system that had become corrupt to its core and was hurting their fellow Americans. These fresh faces with their new ideas and a determination to put power back into the hands of the people were going to inspire American voters to get up and get involved in democracy for maybe the first time ever. The kind of smarmy, win-at-any-cost energy Darrell seemed to bring to our race toward the end was exactly what the #resisters and political newcomers were protesting and fighting against. I've always been a Democrat because I believe we're a party of folks trying to do the right thing. So as awkward as it was, I did the right thing, picked up the phone, and called the frontrunner.

I feel like I need to point out just how amicable and friendly our primary race was because it's something I'm very proud of. I don't know what the norm is in other races, but we didn't really have it out for one another while on the trail. There weren't any scathing attacks at the debates or meanness that I can recall. We even had one another's cell phone numbers and we definitely texted a few times during the primary race. When one of my volunteers turned out to be just shy of being a scary stalker, I let them all know to keep him away from their campaigns. The respect was mutual, too. One time I'd gotten an incorrect address for a candidate event, and they were all happy to send me the correct information as soon as I asked for it. No sabotage or pettiness. I really had a pleasant time on the trail, and I owe a lot of that to the fact that my opponents were pretty decent dudes.

Of course, after my race was over, I'd heard through the grapevine that a fellow candidate had gone around telling folks that I didn't like Black people because, and I shit you not, I believed "Asians were harder workers than Black folks."

During my call with the frontrunner, I tried to be as friendly and helpful as I could. I reassured him that none of us were interested in further spreading this lying nonsense about his family, that we were focused on the issues, and that we each seemed determined to keep this race clean. And, honestly, aside from Darrell's email BS, we all did run an honest and clean race. Even now, I definitely consider these guys my political friends-in-arms.

With his sensible khakis, his salt-and-pepper hair that's never even an inch overgrown, and a booming voice made for breaking up scuffles between angsty teenage athletes on the field, Todd is the amalgamation of every sitcom dad you watched on TV growing up. A moderate dude (in demeanor and politics alike), he wants to bring "common sense and common decency back to D.C."

A few years younger than me, Ali is the Democratic Socialist with the Mostest. I thought I had some chutzpah, but I don't know if I'd have ever opened every stump speech of mine by calling myself the "Bi-racial, Bi-sexual, Biochemist," but he certainly did. And in Texas no less! I credit his Democratic Socialist platform with making sure all the candidates in our race had to speak on and explain their support or lack of support for things like Medicare for All, a living wage, and LGBTQIA rights.

If a golden retriever and yellow lab mix could somehow Frankenstein its brain into the body of a human being, you would have HP. Considering he is from a locally well-known and wealthy family, you'd think he'd be even the tiniest bit snobby or standoffish, but nope. This man would give you the shirt off his back, the food off his plate, and the last twenty dollars in his wallet if he thought you needed it. Very few people deserve to be described as having a heart of gold, but HP definitely has one.

Handsome, with a charming smile and confident swag, Darrell is impossible not to like the moment you see him. After getting to meet him a few times on the campaign trail, and in sharp contrast to the other primary candidates, Darrell sort of came off like he wasn't in this race for all the right reasons. As a candidate running against someone, you start to understand the motivations behind a person's interest in running for office. But with Darrell, it always seemed like he was only half interested in the race, especially with him spending the last five weeks leading up to the primary election in another state.

After the primary, HP, Ali, and I worked together to organize a fundraiser meet and greet for Todd. Our politics didn't fully align with one another, but I do believe that coming together in 2018 in support of the Democratic primary winner was the decent and right thing to do. That midterm election, Houston made history up and down the ballot, electing people that truly represented the diversity of this great city. I believe our race played a role in getting folks out to vote who hadn't voted before. I will forever be grateful and proud to have run alongside such upstanding guys (well, except maybe Darrell), and I'm glad we got to help make our city a little bit better and more civically engaged.

THAT LITTLE
VOICE INSIDE
YOUR HEAD IS
AN *Asshole*

I know it's probably unbecoming for a former U.S. congressional candidate to end the last chapter of her book with swear words. Thankfully, however, propriety and appropriateness have been relegated to yesteryear (or pre-2015), a simpler time in politics (and the world).

Now, Trump is president. The world is on fire, figuratively and literally. At the time of printing we are in the midst of a global pandemic, and so I'd like to believe a few cuss words in my book won't even garner a highly downvoted post on Reddit!

Yay to this new age in politics.

My inner voice is an asshole. Like, right now, I'm sitting at my dining room table, and that asshole in my head is trying its best to convince me I have no idea what the hell I'm doing, and that I should leave the book writing to the *actual* writers out there. And that also, what kind of selfish person publishes and promotes a book in the *middle of a pandemic?!*

Unlike my conscience, which is a kinder, gentler, Jiminy-Cricket-type voice helping me navigate life while encouraging me to be the best person I can, the Asshole has tasked itself with making sure I'm constantly aware of all the things I'm messing up. It's the Tiger Mom I was fortunate enough to never have IRL.

If I had a dollar for every time the Asshole tried to get me to quit during my campaign because "Silky, you're not good enough, smart enough, pedigreed enough, connected enough, polished enough, rich enough (or at all), attractive enough, and certainly not qualified enough to run for congress. You should probably sit this one out and think about trying again in a few years (or decades)," I'd have probably raised enough money to win my primary, and I'd be writing this book from my Congressional office in D.C. *ba dum ts!*

I've got an irritatingly high self-esteem and an unshakable self-worth, but I'd be lying if I didn't admit that a lot of what I do or work toward in life is in spite of this little voice. The good thing is that I'm very stubborn, and I've got issues with authority, so I never let the Asshole boss me around. Nevertheless, the Asshole persists.

When I was younger, I used to wonder if I was the only person with an Asshole for my inner voice. Over the last few years, however, as I've become more open and honest about how hard it can be to believe in myself, I've discovered that I am far from alone in having an Asshole live rent-free in my head. Since my time on the trail, I've continued to meet amazing, brilliant people doing all kinds of amazing, brilliant things in their corners of the world, all of whom talk about their own doubts and wishy-washy belief in themselves.

Because I am my own worst critic, I often find it hard to be proud of myself for the things I've done or accomplished. It's not like I've cured cancer, won a Nobel Peace Prize, solved a Rubik's Cube, or gotten elected to federal office. I haven't even done anything cool enough to warrant a Netflix show about my life! But over the last year, I've realized how unfair I've been to myself. For months I ignored the Asshole in my head constantly telling me to quit my race before I embarrassed myself; I didn't let the possibility of failure scare me off, and I find that pretty damn impressive.

Two years ago, I was the first woman to run in the Democratic Primary for my congressional district. This year, that same race had two women on the primary ballot, and the winner was an immigrant woman of color. All over the country, people are stepping up to defend our democracy. There are so many newbies to politics who are like, "Screw it, I'm just gonna do it," and they're putting their lives on hold to do what they believe is the right, patriotic thing to do. I'd bet dollars to donuts that each and every newbie-nobody who has run for office these last few years has done so in spite of the Asshole inner voice telling them to "sit back down and let the professionals handle it." I am so damn proud to live in a country where nobodies can step up, get their name on the ballot, and have a fighting chance at representing people who look/worship/love just like them.

I ran for office because I wanted to make a difference. I also know that I *could* run for office because of generations of women, men, and POC who ignored their own resident Assholes to do the big, scary, impossible things they knew had to be done. I am so grateful for the privilege of being an American and for getting to be a small part of the history we made as a country in 2018.

Moral of the story? Always stand up for what's right. And when that little voice in your head says you should sit back down, be sure to tell that Asshole to fuck right off.

INSPIRING
Quotes

The opposite of winning isn't losing—
it's failing to see the larger picture.

PICO IYER

Seventy-five percent of who I am comes from my parents, my family, school, my daily horoscope from age thirteen to sixteen (I'm an Aries if you're curious), and *Saturday Night Live* (the Norm Macdonald through Tina Fey years). The other twenty-five percent can be attributed to punk rock and country music lyrics and my time spent devouring any Reader's Digest and *Chicken Soup for the Soul* I could get my hands on as a very impressionable tween. So in an effort to harken back to those halcyon days of the nineties, here are several pages of inspiring quotes, many of which helped me to appreciate the victory in my own defeat.

Winning or losing of the election is less
important than strengthening the country.

INDIRA GANDHI

When I lose a match, I know that
I lose on the court and not in life.

GABRIELA SABATINI

You must accept that you might fail; then, if
you do your best and still don't win, at least you
can be satisfied that you've tried. If you don't
accept failure as a possibility, you don't set high
goals, you don't branch out, you don't try—
you don't take the risk.

ROSALYNN CARTER

Losing is part of the game. If you
never lose, you are never truly tested,
and never forced to grow.

DAVID SIRLIN

If you learn from a loss you have not lost.

AUSTIN O'MALLEY

If you're afraid of losing,
then you daren't win.

BJORN BORG

Winning is great, sure, but if you are really
going to do something in life, the secret is
learning how to lose. Nobody goes undefeated
all the time. If you can pick up after a crushing
defeat, and go on to win again, you are going
to be a champion someday.

WILMA RUDOLPH

Win as if you were used to it, lose
as if you enjoyed it for a change.

RALPH WALDO EMERSON

You have no choices about how you lose,
but you do have a choice about how you
come back and prepare to win again.

PAT RILEY

Losing is only temporary and not
all-encompassing. You must simply study
it, learn from it, and try hard not to lose
the same way again. Then you must have
the self-control to forget about it.

JOHN WOODEN

That's what learning is, after all; not whether
we lose the game, but how we lose and how
we've changed because of it and what we
take away from it that we never had before,
to apply to other games. Losing, in a
curious way, is winning.

RICHARD BACH

I never thought of losing, but now
that it's happened, the only thing is
to do it right. That's my obligation
to all the people who believe in me.
We all have to take defeats in life.

MUHAMMAD ALI

We must accept finite disappointment,
but never lose infinite hope.

MARTIN LUTHER KING, JR.

You can't succeed if you don't
know what losing is.

GARTH BROOKS

Losses have propelled me to even bigger places, so I understand the importance of losing. You can never get complacent because a loss is always around the corner. It's in any game that you're in—a business game or whatever—you can't get complacent.

VENUS WILLIAMS

It's okay to lose. Losing teaches you something. Having to try and going through the trials and tribulations to actually overcome, to get there, to win, to triumph, that's what makes life interesting.

ELIZABETH BANKS

You learn more from losing than winning. You learn how to keep going.

MORGAN WOOTTEN

The greatest test of courage on earth is to bear defeat without losing heart.

ROBERT GREEN INGERSOLL

Winning and losing isn't everything; sometimes, the journey is just as important as the outcome.

ALEX MORGAN

Only those who dare to fail greatly
can ever achieve greatly.

ROBERT F. KENNEDY

Giving up is the only sure way to fail.

GENA SHOWALTER

Failure should be our teacher, not our
undertaker. Failure is delay, not defeat. It is
a temporary detour, not a dead end. Failure
is something we can avoid only by saying
nothing, doing nothing, and being nothing.

DENIS WAITLEY

I have not failed. I've just found
10,000 ways that won't work.

THOMAS A. EDISON

You build on failure. You use it as a
stepping stone. Close the door on the
past. You don't try to forget the mistakes,
but you don't dwell on it. You don't
let it have any of your energy, or any
of your time, or any of your space.

JOHNNY CASH

Success is not final, failure is not fatal: it
is the courage to continue that counts.

WINSTON CHURCHILL

There is only one thing that makes a dream
impossible to achieve: the fear of failure.

PAULO COELHO

We are all failures—at least the best of us are.

J.M. BARRIE

Failures are finger posts on the
road to achievement.

C.S. LEWIS

Winners are not afraid of losing.
But losers are. Failure is part of
the process of success. People who
avoid failure also avoid success.

ROBERT T. KIYOSAKI

I can accept failure, everyone fails at
something. But I can't accept not trying.

MICHAEL JORDAN

No man ever achieved worthwhile success
who did not, at one time or other, find himself
with at least one foot hanging well over the
brink of failure.

NAPOLEON HILL

Our greatest glory is not in never failing,
but in rising every time we fail.

CONFUCIUS

Failure is the condiment that
gives success its flavor.

TRUMAN CAPOTE

Failure is success in progress.

ALBERT EINSTEIN

You may encounter many defeats, but you must
not be defeated. In fact, it may be necessary to
encounter the defeats, so you can know who
you are, what you can rise from, how you can
still come out of it.

MAYA ANGELOU

You'll always miss 100% of
the shots you don't take.

WAYNE GRETZKY

I've missed more than 9,000 shots in my career. I've lost almost 300 games. Twenty-six times, I've been trusted to take the game-winning shot and missed. I've failed over and over and over again in my life. And that is why I succeed.

MICHAEL JORDAN

You can't let your failures define you. You have to let your failures teach you.

BARACK OBAMA

In any case, you must not confuse a single failure with a final defeat.

F. SCOTT FITZGERALD

Do not judge me by my successes; judge me by how many times I fell down and got back up again.

NELSON MANDELA

Think like a queen. A queen is not afraid to fail. Failure is another stepping stone to greatness.

OPRAH WINFREY

Courage allows the successful
woman to fail—and learn powerful
lessons from the failure—o that in
the end, she didn't fail at all.

MAYA ANGELOU

Good people are good because they've come
to wisdom through failure. We get very little
wisdom from success, you know.

WILLIAM SAROYAN

Failure is unimportant. It takes
courage to make a fool of yourself.

CHARLIE CHAPLIN

Don't fear failure—not failure,
but low aim, is the crime. In great
attempts it is glorious even to fail.

BRUCE LEE

What matters is this: being fearless of
failure arms you to break the rules. In doing
so, you may change the culture and just
possibly, for a moment, change life itself.

MALCOLM MCLAREN

If you fell down yesterday, stand up today.

H.G. WELLS

I don't believe in failure. It is not
failure if you enjoyed the process.

OPRAH WINFREY

Failure doesn't kill you… it increases your
desire to make something happen.

KEVIN COSTNER

Failure is a part of [the] process.
You just learn to pick yourself up.
And the quicker and more resilient
you become, the better you are.

MICHELLE OBAMA

I thank God for my failures. Maybe not
at the time but after some reflection.
I never feel like a failure just because
something I tried has failed.

DOLLY PARTON

Failure happens all the time. It happens
every day in practice. What makes
you better is how you react to it.

MIA HAMM

You may be disappointed if you fail,
but you are doomed if you don't try.

BEVERLY SILLS

It is not the critic who counts; not the man who points out how the strong man stumbles, or where the doer of deeds could have done them better. The credit belongs to the man who is actually in the arena, whose face is marred by dust and sweat and blood; who strives valiantly; who errs, who comes short again and again, because there is no effort without error and shortcoming; but who does actually strive to do the deeds; who knows great enthusiasms, the great devotions; who spends himself in a worthy cause; who at the best knows in the end the triumph of high achievement, and who at the worst, if he fails, at least fails while daring greatly, so that his place shall never be with those cold and timid souls who neither know victory nor defeat.

THEODORE ROOSEVELT

ACKNOWLEDGMENTS

When I was young and full of the ignorance and overconfidence that comes with youth, I frequently gave myself nearly ALL the credit for becoming the person I was at that time. Not until I got a little older did I come to realize and appreciate the fact that I am not *just* the product of my own thoughts and feelings and experiences. Not even by a longshot. Instead, and despite several of my less-than-wonderful personality traits, I have somehow managed to build a life surrounded by all kinds of amazing, positive, supportive, and inspiring individuals. During my run for office, I got to further add to my own village of teachers and hype-people, and I would be remiss if I didn't give the friends I made on the trail a shout-out for building me up and believing in me. I recognize how lucky I am to have had the privilege to run for office with such an incredible amount of love, positivity, and support in my corner. My experience could have been negative or disheartening, but instead, I got to grow as a person and meet some incredibly kind and beautiful souls along the way.

Originally, I attempted to list out each and every person who gave their time, energy and support to my campaign. After getting to the fiftieth person on my list I started stressing over the thought of leaving someone out, so I'm going to play it safe, and give a broad thank you to all y'all who have made my world a little bit brighter since we've met, both during my campaign and after.

Whether it was working or volunteering on my campaign week after week, helping me turn this book into a reality through dozens of hours of editing, chatting with me several times a week so I could pick your consultant-brain for free, teaching me how to fundraise, block walking weekend after weekend in the sweltering Texas heat, writing postcards at my dining table, showing up to event after evernt to hype me up, making boring calls day in and day out, handing pushcards out at the polls, opening your home or bar or tribrid art gallery/interior design showroom/furniture store and introducing me to your own friends and family, I appreciate you. Just giving me a knowing wink or nudge on the arm that "you're doing GREAT!" and sending me all your good juju for months on end, made all the difference, and I appreciate that, too. I couldn't have accomplished anything without y'all cheering me on the whole time. You made my run for office a life-changing experience, so from the bottom of my heart, thank you.

I would like to say a special thank you to a few other folks.

Mom and Shane—Oh! How wonderful the world would be if everyone was as loved by their family as I am by mine. Thank you for always being in my corner and for helping me to become who I am. I love you both more than you'll ever know.

Tassrun Nazreen and Asif Malik—Did I hit the in-law jackpot or what?! Your continued faith and support in me all these years is a blessing and a privilege I am grateful for each day. I am so lucky to have a mother and father-in-law who love me like their own daughter.

Daniel J. Cohen and Alex Oriani, RedShift Writers—I wonder if the next time we work on a book together I'll be less combative over keeping every adverb, comma splice and semi-colon y'all want to nix (LOL UNLIKELY)? Also, y'all are stuck with me for life now. #SorryNotSorry

For more stylish and inspiring photos about Silky
and current goings-on in Silky's life,
visit her website at **SilkyJMalik.com**,
or follow her on social media at **Silky_Joshi_Malik**

Made in the USA
Las Vegas, NV
27 November 2022